Sara Nephew

quilts of PRAISE

9 Projects Featuring 3-D Cross and Church Blocks

C&T PUBLISHING
Another Maker Inspired!

Publisher: Amy Barrett-Daffin

Creative Director: Gailen Runge

Senior Editor: Roxane Cerda

Editor: Madison Moore, Marci Baker

Technical Editor: Debbie Rodgers, Gailen Runge

Cover/Book Designer: April Mostek

Production Coordinator: Tim Manibusan

Illustrators: Tim Manibusan, Sara Nephew, and Zinnia Heinzmann

Photography Coordinator: Lauren Herberg

Photography Assistant: Gabriel Martinez

Photography by Lauren Herberg of C&T Publishing, Inc., unless otherwise noted

Published by C&T Publishing, Inc., P.O. Box 1456, Lafayette, CA 94549

Library of Congress Cataloging-in-Publication Data

Names: Nephew, Sara, author.
Title: Quilts of praise : 9 projects featuring 3-D cross and church blocks / Sara Nephew.
Description: Lafayette : C&T Publishing, [2022] | Summary: "Create devotional three-dimensional quilt blocks showcasing crosses and churches perfect for special occasions like weddings, christenings, memorials, and more! Readers will follow along with guides on cutting directions, creating templates, and working with value to develop attractive three-dimensional illusions"-- Provided by publisher.
Identifiers: LCCN 2022036250 | ISBN 9781644032770 (trade paperback) | ISBN 9781644032787 (ebook)
Subjects: LCSH: Quilting--Patterns. | Patchwork--Patterns.
Classification: LCC TT835 .N4584 2022 | DDC 746.46/041--dc23/eng/20220819
LC record available at https://lccn.loc.gov/2022036250

Printed in the USA

10 9 8 7 6 5 4 3 2 1

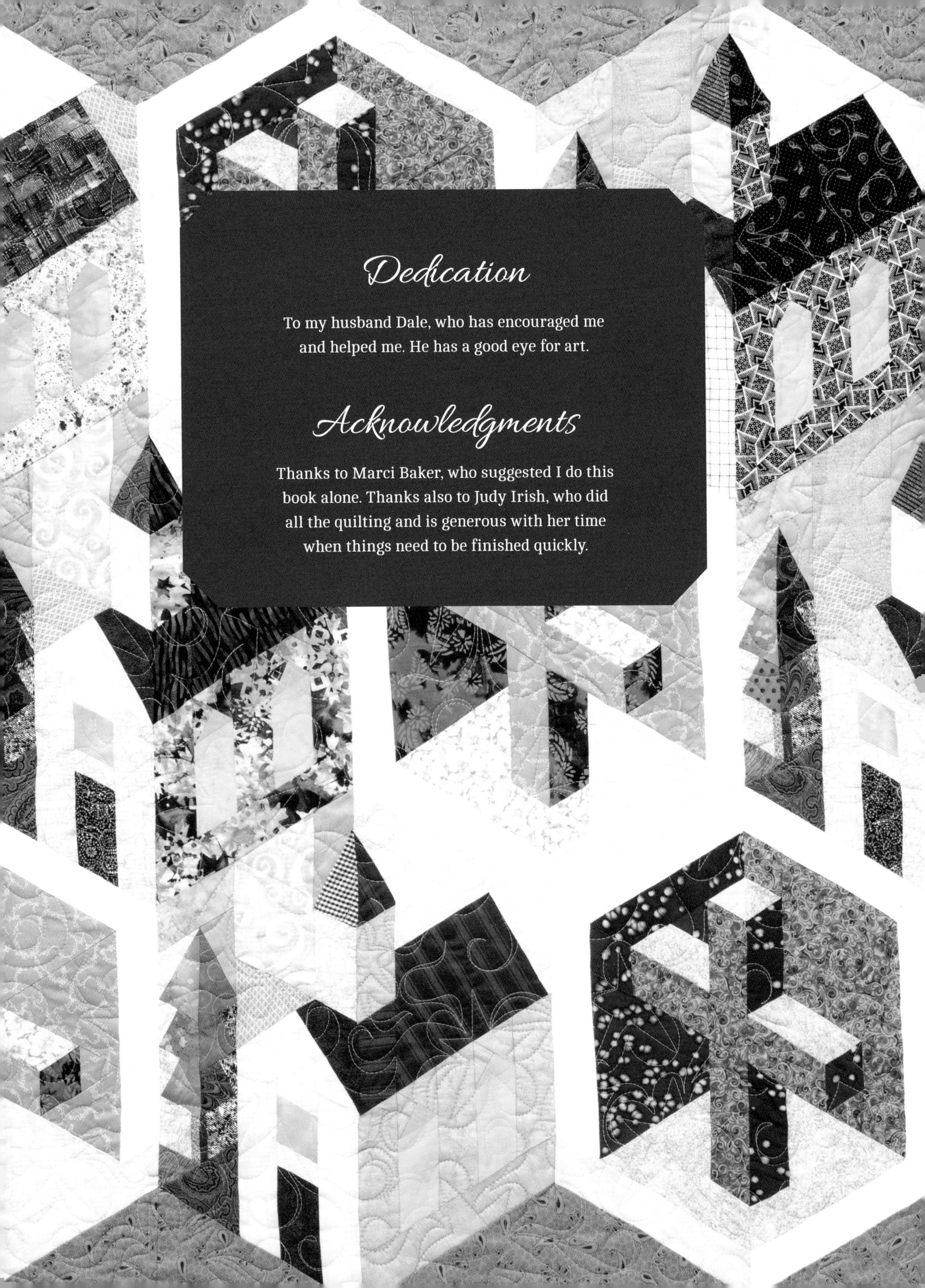

Dedication

To my husband Dale, who has encouraged me and helped me. He has a good eye for art.

Acknowledgments

Thanks to Marci Baker, who suggested I do this book alone. Thanks also to Judy Irish, who did all the quilting and is generous with her time when things need to be finished quickly.

CONTENTS

PROJECTS

Merry Christmas,
Holy Christmas Quilt
(Church in the Woods Quilt) **38**

Monastery Wall Hanging **41**

Medieval Quilt **44**

Three Block Table Runner **47**

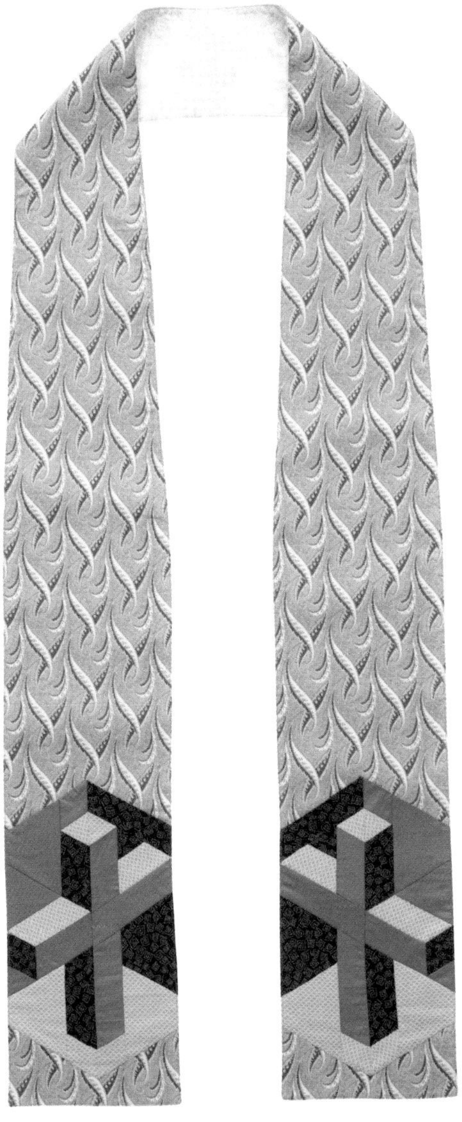

Liturgical Stole **53**

3-D Cross Banner **50**

Introduction

This is a book of quilt patterns with very special meanings. Quilts are made to add bright colors to a room, to wrap soft warmth around a person, to save money by using scraps, and to explore design and color with a sewing machine, among many other things. There's already so much fun involved in choosing a pattern, colors, and fabrics, bringing out the rotary cutter, scissors, and needles. Yet the graphic symbolism of church and cross patterns uncovers even more thoughts and feelings. These quilts may evoke thoughts about deep family bonds and even the meanings of life and death or right and wrong. I feel that it's good to be able to express these things in a familiar, comfortable way. These patterns make perfect, special quilts for a wedding, a first communion, or a get well present. They are gifts with extra love and meaning.

Inspiration

I have been a quilter for a long time. I have developed many different designs and tools, which has created the opportunity for me to travel and teach quilting. This is a wonderful way to meet lots of other quilters.

Fifteen or twenty years ago, in Des Moines, Iowa, a student in my Speedy 3-D class asked for a favor. Her husband was studying to be a deacon and she wanted to make him a stole for the upcoming ceremony. This garment is like a long flat scarf that hangs down in front, with both ends almost to the knee. She was struggling with finding a design to put on each end of the stole. Her friend in class said, "Ask Sara to draw you a 3-D cross!" After some effort, the cross was almost there, but I could not get it quite right. It was sort of floating unattached to anything. It looked strange.

Now, almost twenty years later, I've suddenly gotten it right. The human mind works in mysterious ways. Combining the 3-D cross with the *Church in the Woods* pattern, a group of quilt patterns was born. I bring both here for you to use for personal gifts, important events, and the people most important to you.

Fabrics to Use

To make these blocks, use blouse-weight cotton, prewashed. I have been collecting cotton fabrics since 1989 or so—at quilt shops, garage sales, in old swatch books given out free at drapery stores, from thrift stores, and by trading with friends. I even have fabrics from around the world. I have smaller pieces folded into various rectangles and layered into plastic shoe boxes, with the colored, patterned edges easy to see. When I start a project, it's so much fun to pull out the shoe boxes and consider all the choices.

So naturally, I like to use many different fabrics in one project. I like the scrappy look. Why use just one purple when you have three? By doing this, you can achieve a rich, light-dappled look. But maybe you don't have as many shoe boxes to choose from. Or maybe you prefer to keep the design simple and strong. You only need three fabrics to get started: a light, a medium, and a dark. Batiks and solids work well, and you'll find that in some cases they make cutting easier because you can use both sides while cutting one shape.

CHOOSE THREE VALUES

It's crucial to have fabric in three distinct values—light, medium, and dark—to achieve the special 3-D illusion of these blocks. The light or darkness of the fabric, ignoring the hue, is called *value.* I'm going to share some tricks and techniques that help you judge value between different hues. Learning these skills will make all your quilts more beautiful.

Squint

This one is simple. You know how to do it, and here is a new way to use it. Squinch up your eyes until they are almost closed—almost like a very angry look. This lets less light into your eyes, so everything looks a little bit darker. Lay your fabric candidates next to each other and squint. You will see whether they blend into each other or stand out from one another.

Do it carefully. Unfold the fabric so the thickness doesn't cast a shadow or distract you. Lay the edge of one fabric slightly over the edge of the next in the order of light, medium, and then dark. Squint at the three fabrics. Ideally, they should be evenly distant in value. Like stairs. You don't want stairs where one is barely a step up and the next one is extra tall. You'd be stumbling up the steps!

Squinting also will make small prints blend together, so you notice the value more and the details less. In other cases, squinting will subtract from the impact of hot colors like red, yellow, and some purples, making it easier to judge the value.

Use the squinting method to determine if the light, medium, and dark are equally distant.

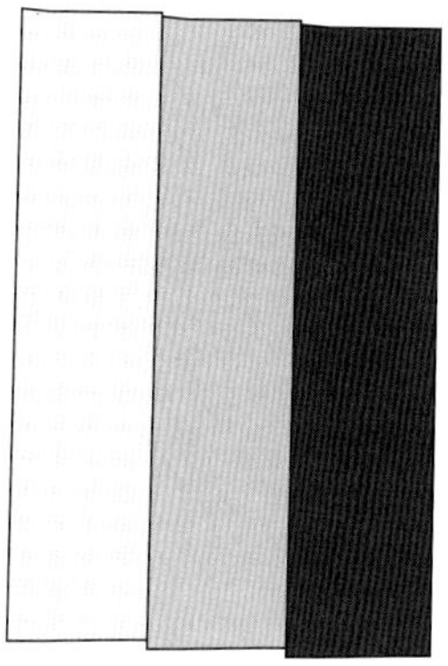

Three equally distant values

Move Fabric Around

After making your choices while squinting at the fabric from light to dark, take your three pieces of fabric and try different positions for the fabric while you squint. Put light and dark next to each other, then lay the medium sideways across, so you can see whether the distance between them is balanced. Don't forget to squint.

The Wings Effect

If you have a medium value that is closer to the dark value than the light value, the light shape stands out and the darks will blend together. On a cube, this looks like wings. If you have a medium value closer to the light value than the dark value, then the dark stands out, and the lights blend together: wings again. We want to avoid this. If you have a very light light, and a very dark dark, try to get a medium that is equally in between. Practice makes it easier.

Light wings and dark wings

If you have one set of colors that produces a strong 3-D effect, it will help carry the illusion in other sets. In this cube, the values are equally distant from each other, which produces the effect we want.

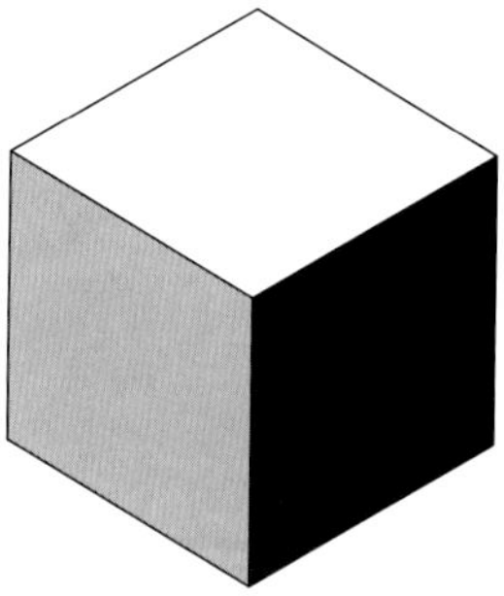

3-D cube

What Not to Use

Do not use high-contrast large prints. They will break up the shapes you cut and destroy the 3-D illusion. Do not use all jewel-toned batiks, even though they're such beautiful colors, and people love them! They are all mediums, so you need lights and darks to go with them, or they will blend into each other, no matter what color they are. Color adds to your design structure like seasoning to food. Color is sweet, sour, hot, or peppery, but does not provide dimensional structure without varying value.

I once saw a woman hand quilting a baby quilt during a church meeting. Up close, the fabric was light pink and light green. But when you were three steps away, the block patterns disappeared, and it all looked as light as a pale sheet.

Lights and darks will provide contrast for your design to stand out. Add medium tones for depth and color. The combination of all three will make your eyes travel around your composition and enjoy the trip. Your quilts will glow!

Cutting Directions

For more information, see *Not Your Grandmother's Log Cabin*, 2nd edition, by Sara Nephew and Marci Baker.

Index of Shapes

These cutting methods are based on cutting a strip of fabric and then using the 60° ruler to cut a particular shape. Each shape is easy to cut as long as you keep in mind the relationship of the triangle ruler to the strip. Here is an overview of the shapes used in this book. Use it as a reference once you are familiar with the cuts.

Triangle page 11

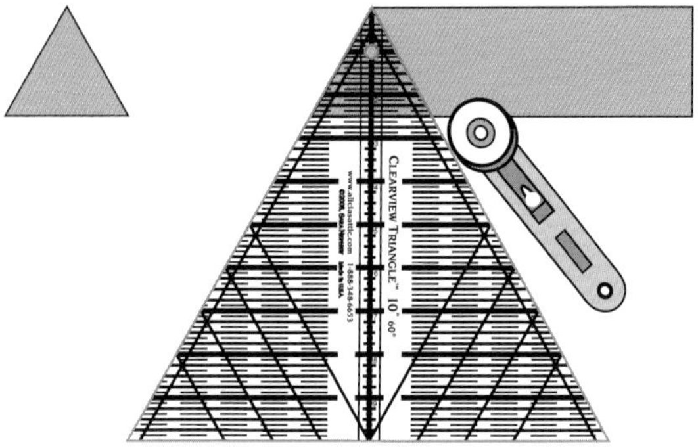

Diamond page 12

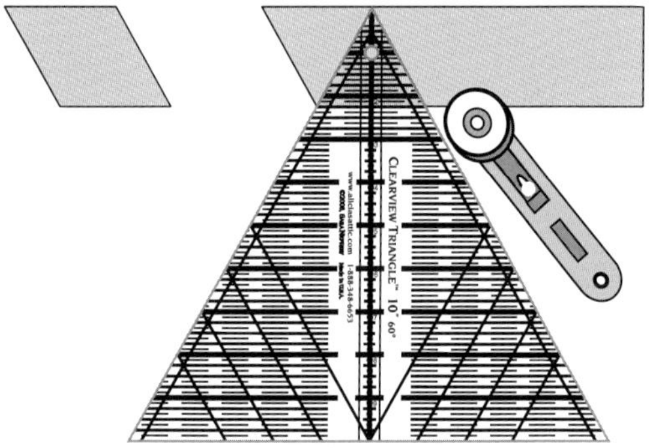

Flat Pyramid page 12

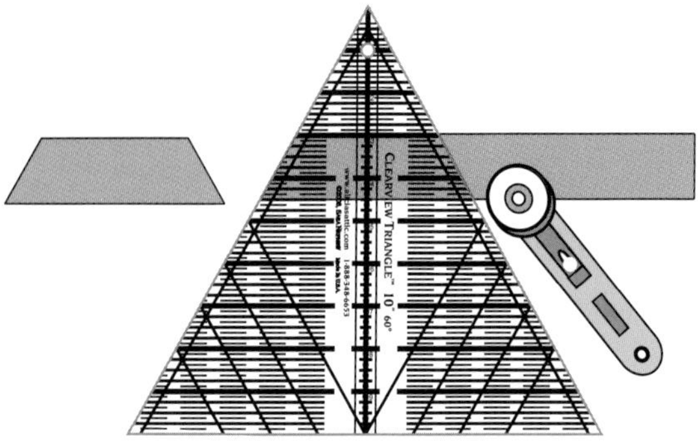

Long Diamond page 13

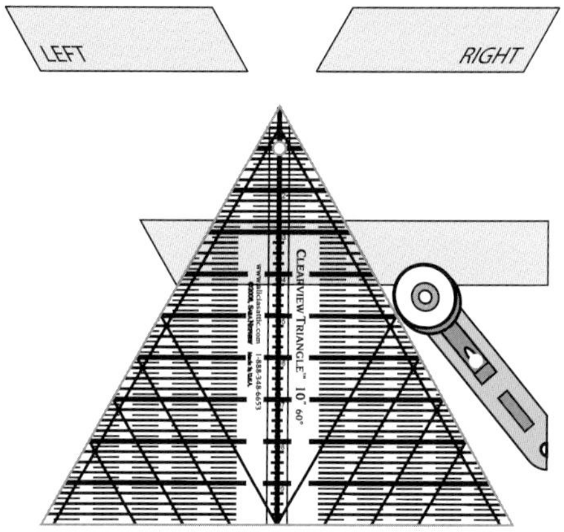

Triangle Half page 14

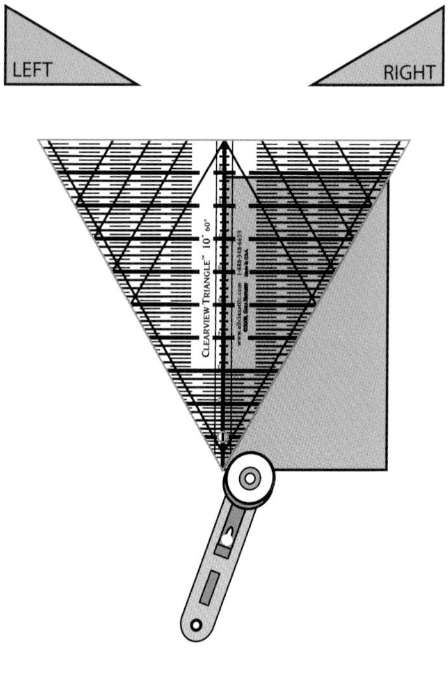

Tools to Use

Clearview Triangles (from C&T Publishing) are 60° rulers that make it simple to cut all the 60° shapes used in these patterns. I use the 10″ ruler the most, and I find the Clearview Triangle Mini Super 60 easy to grab for the very small pieces and especially useful to cut a small diamond half. The full size Clearview Triangle Super 60 is like a combination of these two rulers. The 12″ ruler can also come in handy for a large piece. If you do not have a 60° ruler, you can use the template patterns on pages 57–62.

You will also need a cutting mat and a straightedge ruler or two. A 12″ × 8″ ruler is very useful for cutting strips, and a 24″ × 6″ can trim the quilt edge straight before you put on the binding.

Triangle

1. Cut a 2½″ strip (or a strip the size of the cut triangle).

2. At the right end of the strip, position the ruler with one side along one edge of the strip. Cut the end of the strip to a 60° angle.

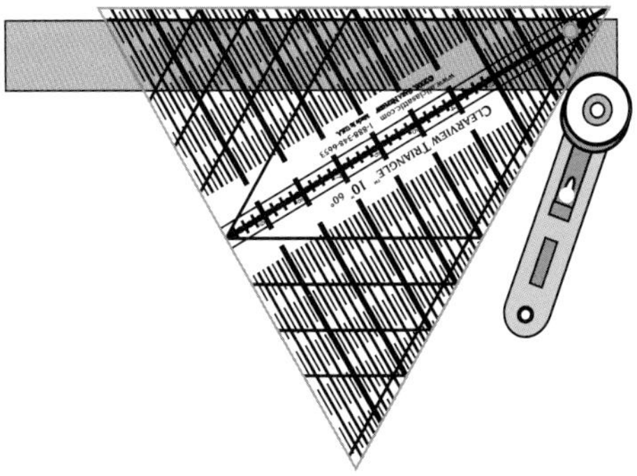

3. Rotate the strip so the cut end is to the left. Position the tip of the ruler at a corner of the strip and the line noted in the pattern at the edge opposite the corner. Cut along the right side. Check with the actual size template (page 57).

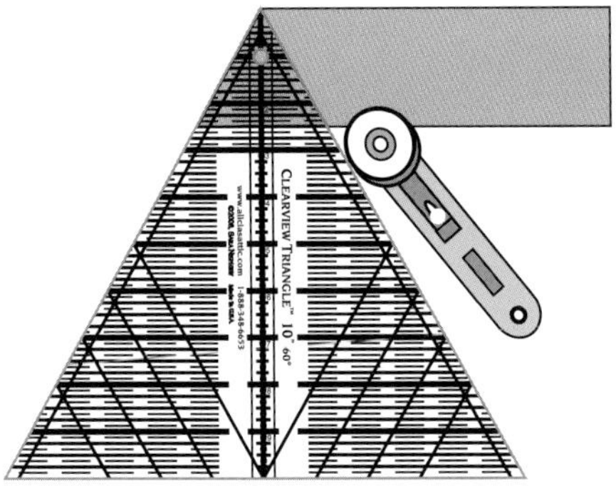

4. For the next triangle, rotate the ruler, aligning the point and appropriate rule line, and rotary cut on the right side.

SPEED CUTTING TRIANGLES

My favorite method requires cutting with both hands or arranging the strip so that cutting is controlled. Caution: Do not attempt this if you are not comfortable cutting with both hands or find that you are cutting toward yourself.

1. Cut a strip the width noted in the pattern.

2. At either end of the strip, position the tip of the ruler at one edge of the strip and the line of the size noted in the pattern at the other edge of the strip.

3. Rotary cut along both sides of the triangle.

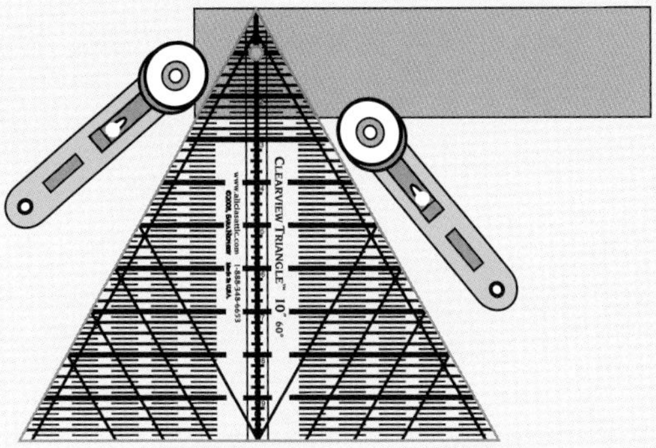

Move the tool along the same edge (do not flip it to the other side of the fabric strip) for the next cut. Align the point, appropriate ruler line, and the edge of the ruler with the corner.

4. Cut along both sides of the triangle.

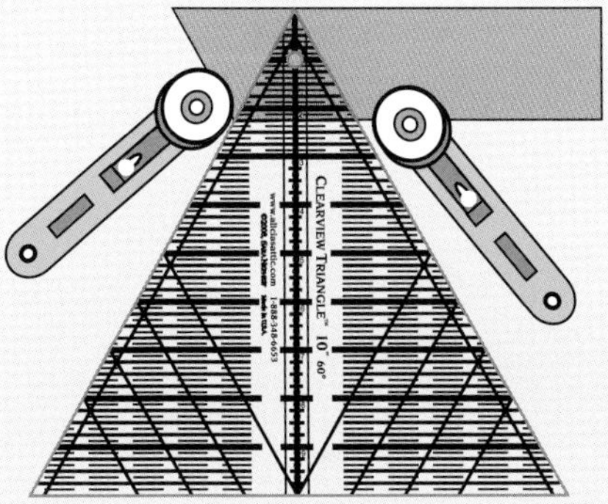

Strips may be stacked up to 6 thicknesses and all cut at once.

Diamond

1. Cut a strip the width noted in the pattern.

2. At the right end of the strip, position the ruler with one side along one edge of the strip. Cut the end of the strip to a 60° angle.

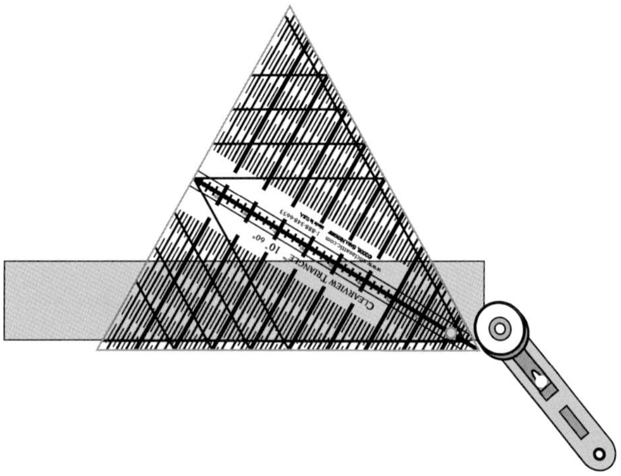

3. Rotate the strip so the cut end is to the left. Place the ruler so the tip is at one edge of the strip, the line of the size noted in the pattern is along the other edge, and the edge of the ruler is at the corner of the cut end.

4. Rotary cut *only* along the side opposite the first cut. Check with the actual size template (page 59).

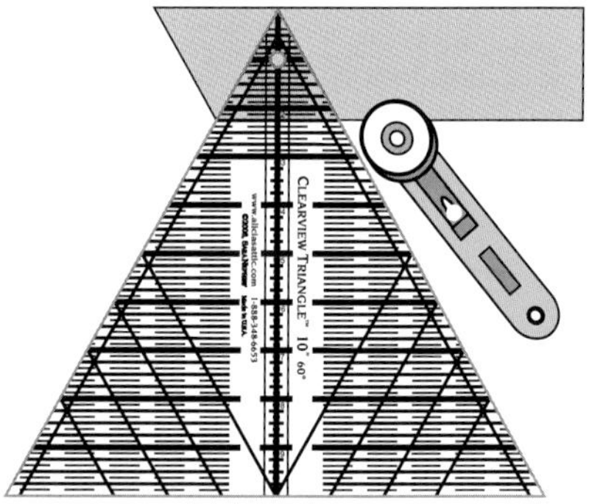

5. Keep moving the tool along the same side of the strip, lining up the cut edge and the side of the tool as shown. Always cut the side opposite the first cut. Strips may be stacked up to 6 thicknesses and all cut at once.

Flat Pyramid

1. Cut the strip width as required in the pattern.

2. At the right end of the strip, position the ruler with one side along one edge of the strip. Cut the end of the strip to a 60° angle.

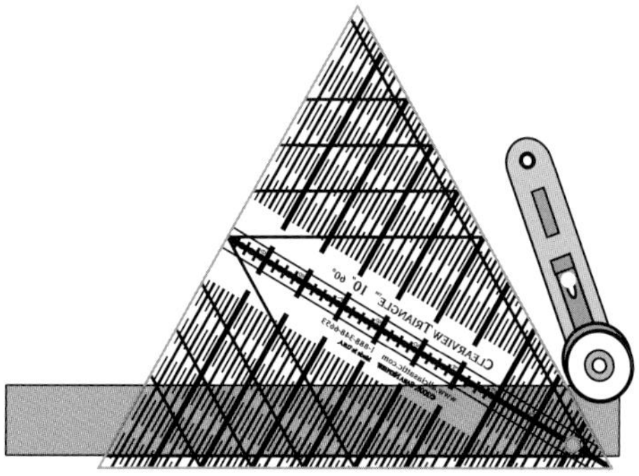

3. Rotate the strip so the cut end is to the left. Align the ruler with the edge along the cut end and the size of the flat pyramid along the bottom edge of the strip.

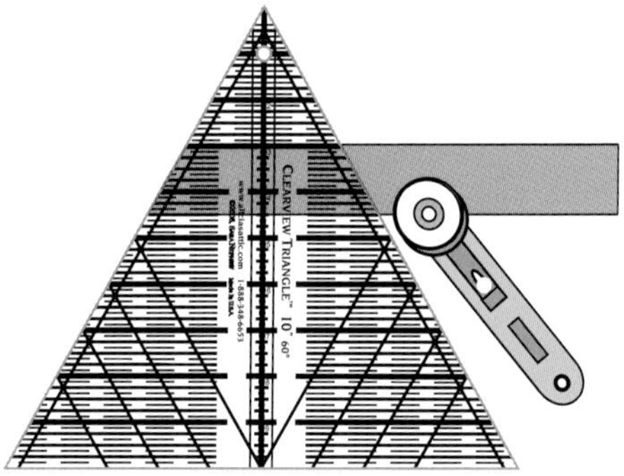

4. Cut along the right side. Check your piece with the actual size templates (pages 58, 59, 60, or 62).

5. Turn the ruler and cut the next flat pyramid from the other side of the strip with the size of the flat pyramid along the top edge.

Long Diamonds

Long diamonds have a reverse of their shape. Check carefully to be sure you are cutting them in the direction required by the pattern. To cut faster, stack the strips all right side up for a particular size and fabric before cutting. Also, long diamonds may be cut from folded fabric if the design includes a long diamond and its reverse from the same fabric.

LEFT (LEANS TO THE LEFT)

1. Cut the strip width as required in the pattern.

2. At the right end of the strip, position the ruler with one side along the bottom edge of the strip. Cut the end of the strip to a 60° angle.

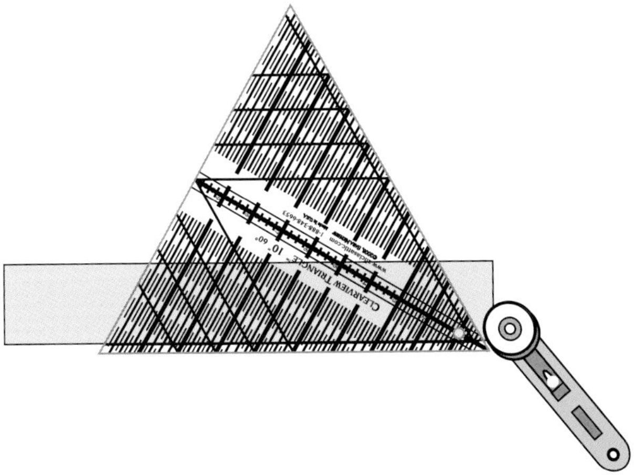

3. Turn the strip so the cut end is to the left. Place the ruler point up with edge at the inside corner and the size of the long diamond along the bottom edge of the strip.

4. Cut *only* along the right side. Check your piece with the actual-size template (page 61).

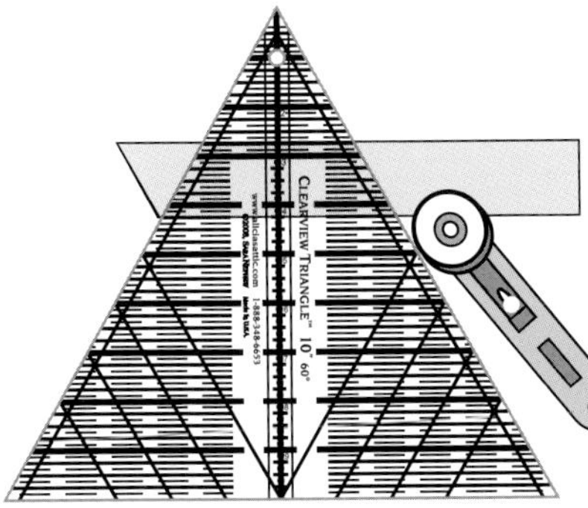

5. Position your ruler the same way for additional long diamonds.

RIGHT (LEANS TO THE RIGHT)

1. Cut the strip width as required in the pattern.

2. At the right end of the strip, position the ruler with one side along the top edge of the strip. Cut the end of the strip to a 60° angle.

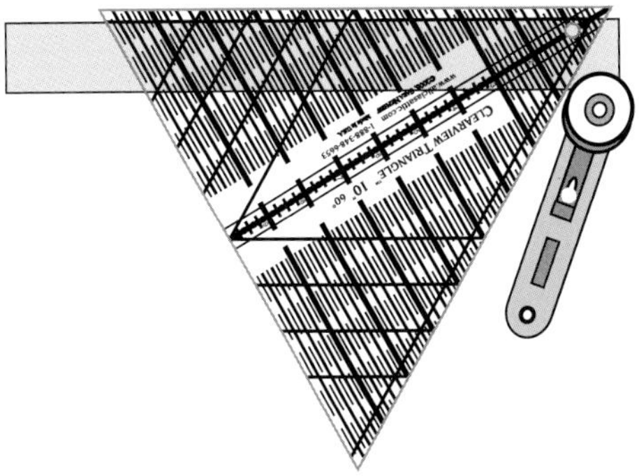

3. Turn the strip so the cut end is to the left. Place the ruler point down with edge at the inside corner and the size of the long diamond along the top edge of the strip.

4. Cut *only* along the right side. Check your piece with the actual-size template (page 58).

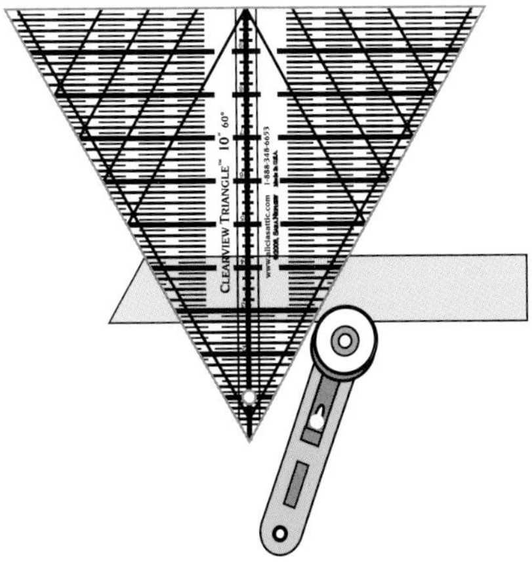

5. Position your ruler the same way for additional long diamonds.

Triangle Half

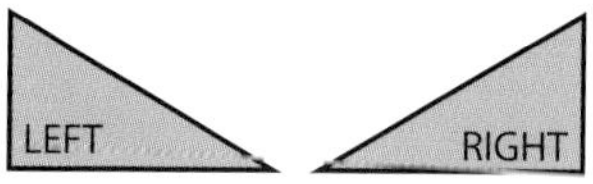

To get left and right halves at the same time, place 2 rectangles, either right or wrong sides together, and cut left or right.

1. Cut a rectangle the height and width needed for the triangle half as given in the directions.

2. Left: With the rectangle vertical and the centerline of the ruler along the left edge of the rectangle and the tip at the lower left corner, cut the rectangle from corner to corner diagonally.

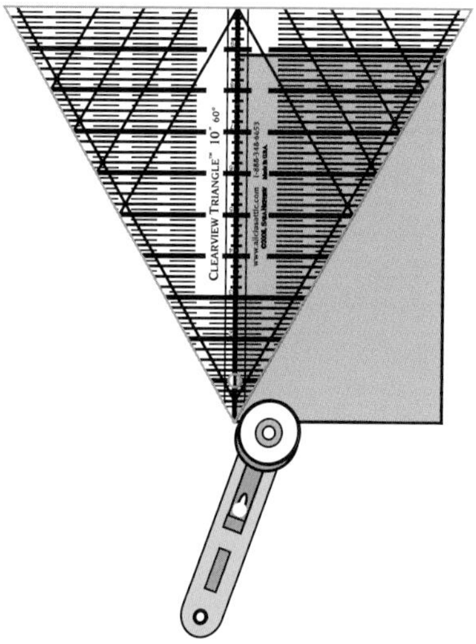

Right: With the rectangle vertical and the centerline of the ruler along the left edge of the rectangle and the tip at the upper left corner, cut the rectangle from corner to corner diagonally.

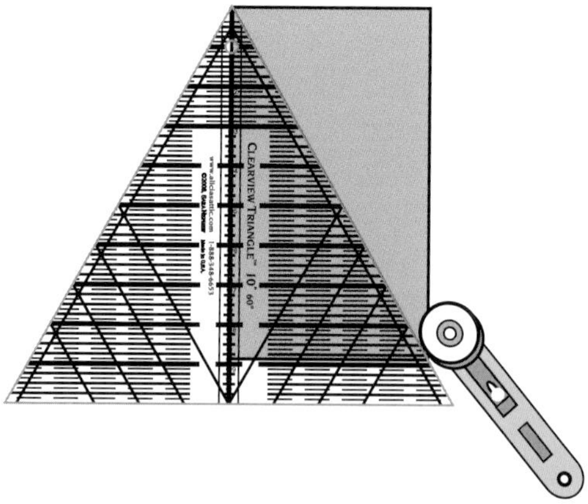

Check your piece with the templates (page 62).

Making the Blocks

3-D Cross Block

This block can be made in two sizes based on a 2″ or 3″ triangle. The 2″ triangle small block measures 10½″ × 13⅝″ with seam allowance. The 3″ triangle large block measures 18½″ × 24¼″ block with seam allowance. (Measurements based on the 3″ triangle appear in parentheses in the directions.)

Make left and right half-blocks separately. Do not sew center seam.

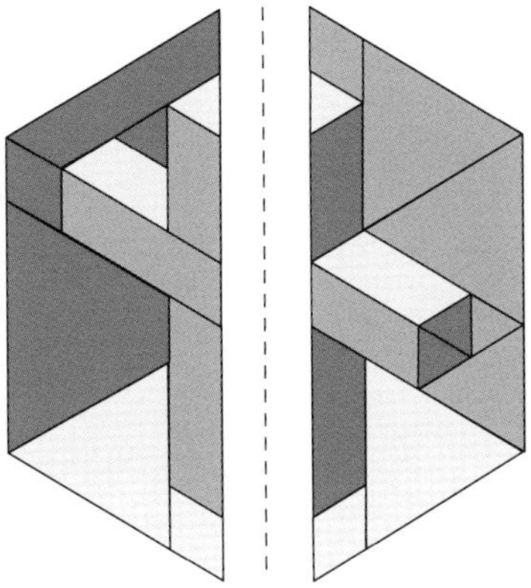

FABRIC

Light:
¼ yard (⅜ yard)

Medium:
¼ yard (¼ yard)

Dark:
¼ yard (⅜ yard)

3-D Cross Left Half-Block

CUTTING LIST FOR ONE LEFT HALF-BLOCK

LIGHT

Qty	Size	Shape
1	2″ (3″)	triangle
1	4½″ (7½″)	triangle
1	1¾″ (2¾″)	diamond
1	3¼″ (5¼″)	flat pyramid cut from a 1¾″ (2¾″) strip

MEDIUM

Qty	Size	Shape
1	3″ (5″)	right long diamond cut from a 1¾″ (2¾″) strip
1 each	4¼″ (7¼″)	right and left long diamond cut from a 1¾″ (2¾″) strip

DARK

Qty	Size	Shape
1	2″ (3″)	triangle
1	1¾″ (2¾″)	diamond
1	5¾″ (9¾″)	flat pyramid cut from a 1¾″ (2¾″) strip
1	5¾″ (9¾″)	flat pyramid cut from a 4¼″ (7¼″) strip

Make the Block

Tip

When making multiple blocks, cut in quantity for speedy piecing.

1. According to the diagram: sew the 5¾″ (9¾″) dark flat pyramid to the 4½″ (7½″) light triangle. Sew the 4¼″ (7¼″) medium right long diamond to the 1¾″ (2¾″) light diamond. Sew the two together. Then sew the 4¼″ (7¼″) medium left long diamond to the 1¾″ (2¾″) dark diamond. Add this strip to the top of the other combined shapes.

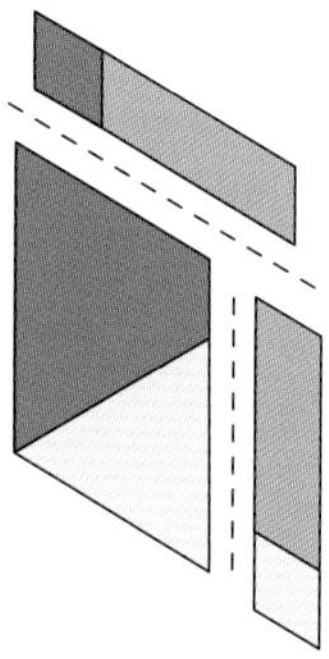

Cross left half-block bottom section

2. Sew the left half-block top section. According to the diagram: sew the 3¼″ (5¼″) light flat pyramid to the 2″ (3″) dark triangle. Sew the 3″ (5″) medium right long diamond to the 2″ (3″) light triangle. Sew the two together as shown. Then sew the 5¾″ (9¾″) dark flat pyramid to them top left.

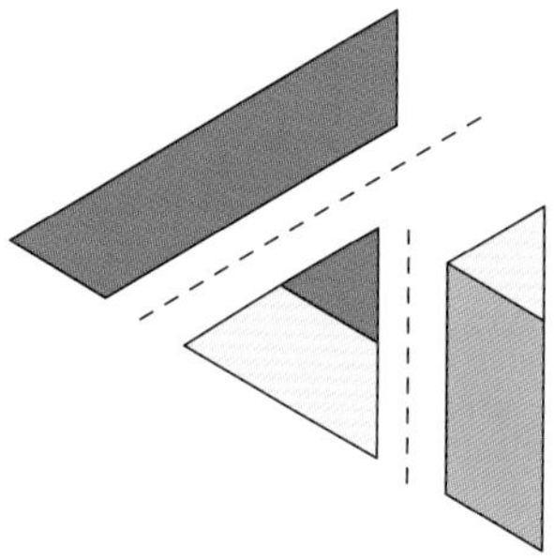

Cross left half-block top section

3. According to the diagram: sew both sections together to complete the left half-block.

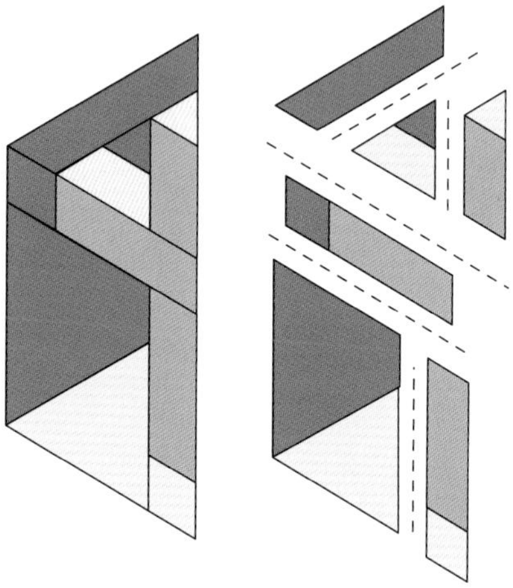

Cross left half-block

Left and Right Long Diamonds

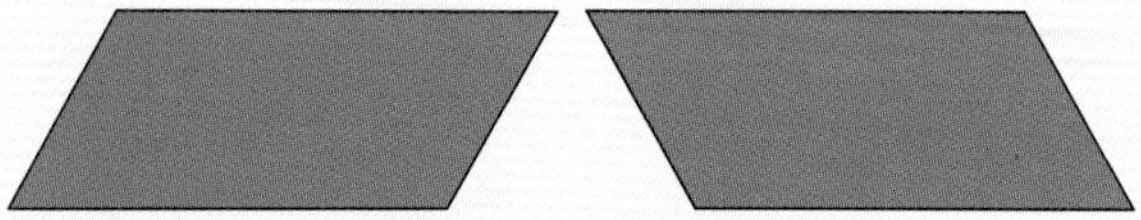

Left and right long diamonds

Be aware that the ends of a long diamond may be cut left or right, so check which you are cutting and which the pattern requires. If the pattern requires the reverse (same fabric) in the other half-block, you can fold the strip on itself and cut both left and right at the same time. And if you are cutting batik or a total solid, you can cut a stack and simply turn the piece over to get the required angle.

3-D Cross Right Half-Block

CUTTING LIST FOR ONE RIGHT HALF-BLOCK

LIGHT

Qty	Size	Shape
1	2″ (3″)	triangle
1	4½″ (7½″)	triangle
1	1¾″ (2¾″)	diamond
1	3″ (5″)	right long diamond cut from a 1¾″ (2¾″) strip

MEDIUM

Qty	Size	Shape
1	2″ (3″)	triangle
1	3¼″ (5¼″)	triangle
2	4½″ (7½″)	triangle
1	1¾″ (2¾″)	diamond
1	3″ (5″)	left long diamond cut from a 1¾″ (2¾″) strip

DARK

Qty	Size	Shape
2	2″ (3″)	triangle
1	4½″ (7½″)	flat pyramid cut from a 1¾″ (2¾″) strip
1	3″ (5″)	left long diamond cut from a 1¾″ (2¾″) strip

1. According to the diagram: sew the dark flat pyramid to the light diamond. Sew this strip to the 4½″ (7½″) light triangle.

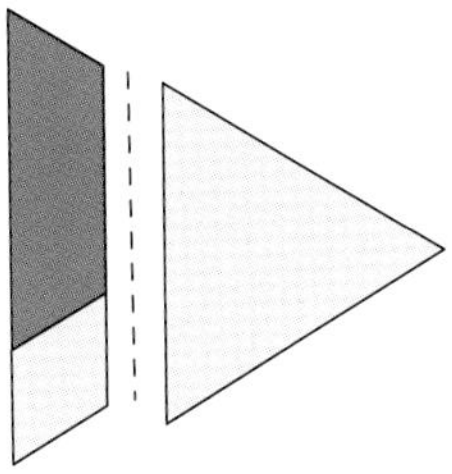

Cross right half-block bottom section

2. According to the diagram: sew the 3″ (5″) medium left long diamond to a 2″ (3″) dark triangle. Sew the 3″ (5″) light right long diamond to a (2″) 3″ dark triangle, adding a medium triangle last to the strip. Sew the two strips together as shown. Sew the 3¼″ (5¼″) medium triangle on the right end of this group. Then sew a 4½″ (7½″) medium triangle at top right.

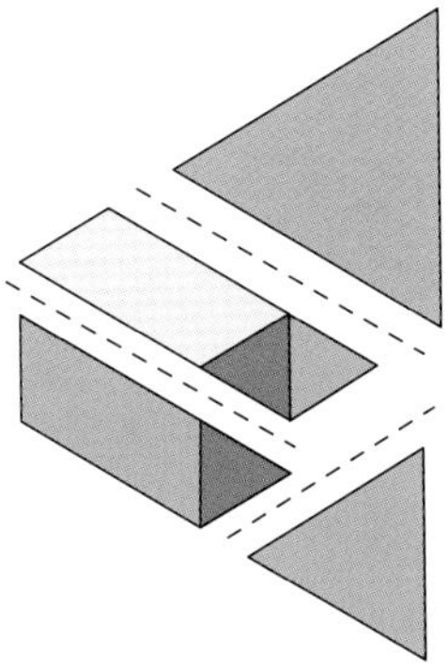

Cross right half-block middle section

3. According to the diagram: sew the 3″ (5″) dark left long diamond to a light triangle. Add a medium diamond as shown. Sew this strip to the 4½″ (7½″) medium triangle.

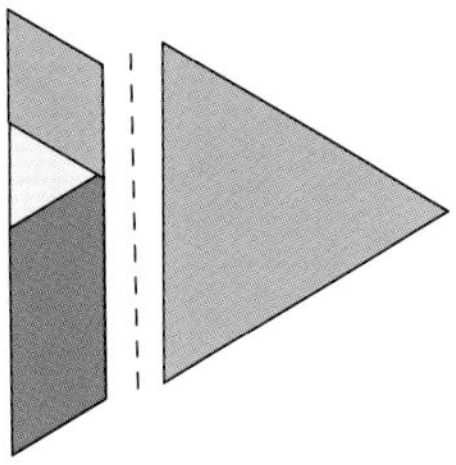

Cross right half-block top section

4. According to the diagram: assemble the three sections to make the cross right half-block.

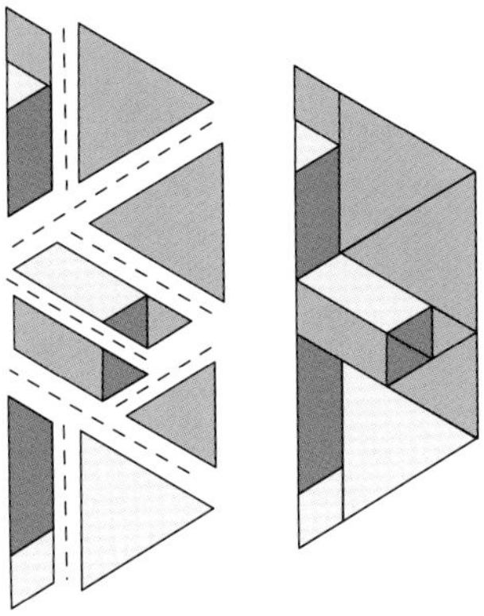

Cross right half-block

Framed Cross Block

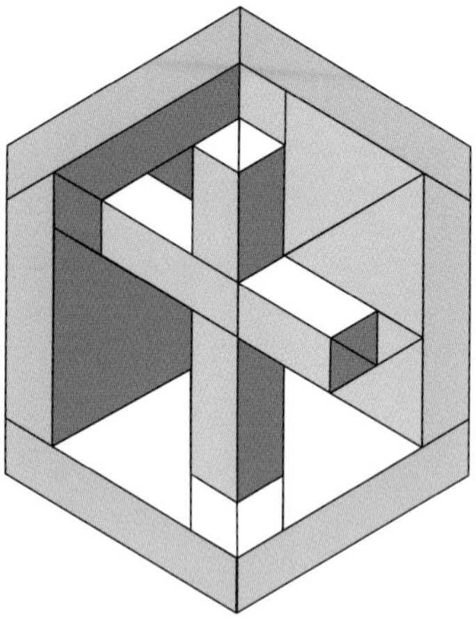

FABRIC

Frame: ⅛ yard

1. Prepare a small 3-D cross left half-block and a small 3-D cross right half-block.

2. Sew the 7″ flat pyramids onto the flat left and right sides of each half-block as shown. Then sew the 6¾″ left and right long diamonds onto the top and bottom sides to complete the half-frames. Do not sew the half-blocks together until you are putting the quilt top together.

CUTTING LIST FOR FRAME

Qty	Size	Shape
2	7″	flat pyramid cut from a 1¾″ strip
2	6¾″	left long diamond cut from a 1¾″ strip
2	6¾″	right long diamond cut from a 1¾″ strip

Quick Cutting

Framing a block or fill-in piece is so quick. You don't even have to use a batik or solid to double-cut your frame. The 7″ flat pyramid is the same in both directions, so you can cut folded fabric and each piece works. The piece you are framing uses a left long diamond on one side and a right on the other, so you'll get exactly what you'll need out of your folded 1¾″ strip.

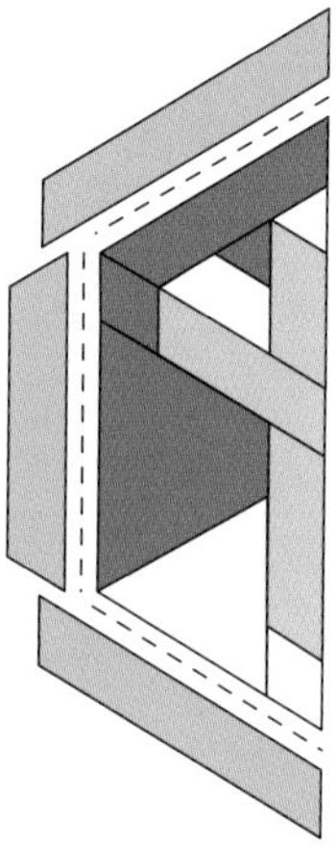

Piecing left framed half-block

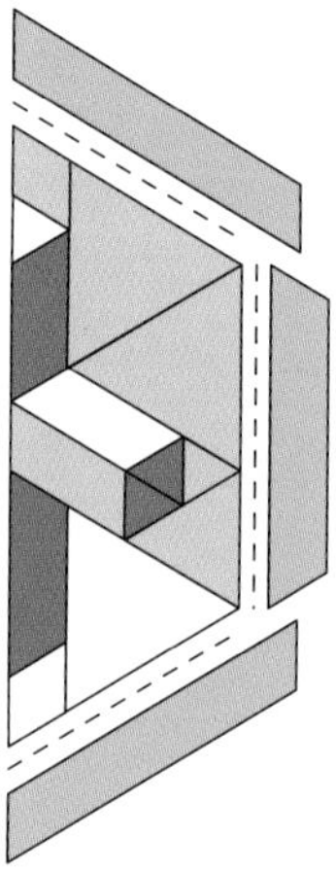

Piecing right framed half-block

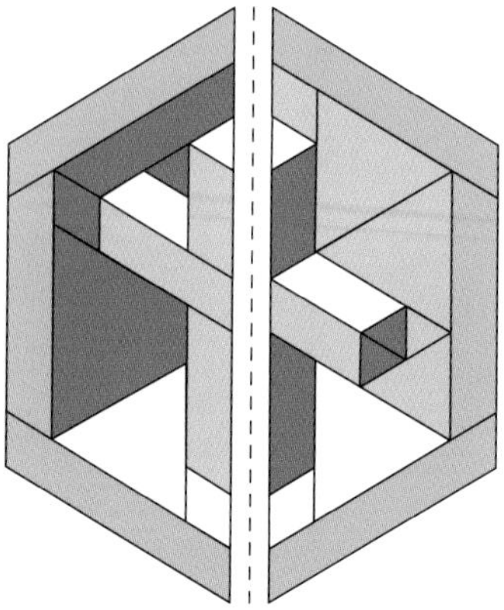

Finished framed cross block with half-blocks separate

Framed Fill-in Piece

FABRIC

Fill-in piece: ¼ yard

Frame: ⅛ yard

CUTTING LIST

Qty & Piece	Size	Shape
1 fill-in	5½″ × 14″	rectangle; trim ends to 60° (see step 1)
1 frame	7″	flat pyramid cut from a 1¾″ strip
1 frame	6¾″	left long diamond cut from a 1¾″ strip
1 frame	6¾″	right long diamond cut from a 1¾″ strip

1. Use a Clearview Triangle 60° ruler to trim off the left and right ends of the 5½″ × 14″ fill-in rectangle to 60° angles as shown.

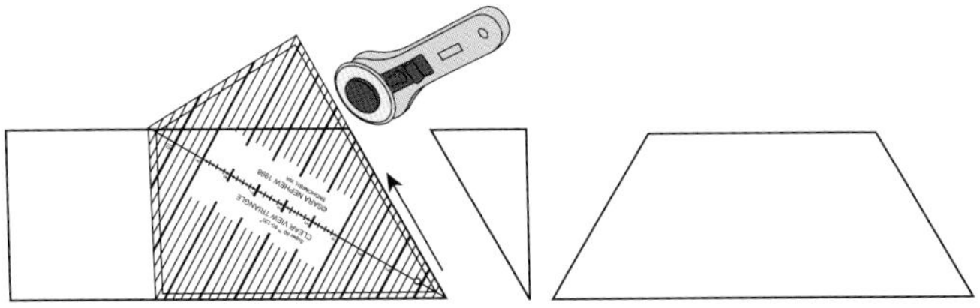

Trimming fill-in piece

2. Sew a 7″ flat pyramid of framing fabric onto fill-in piece as shown. Then sew on a 6¾″ long diamond to the left and right sides to complete the frame.

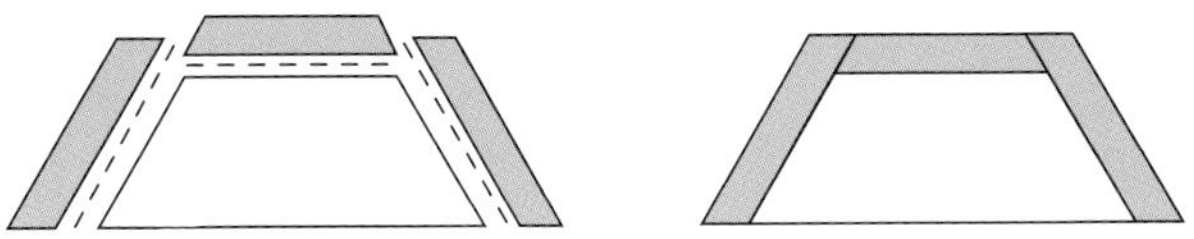

Sewing on framing pieces

Framed fill-in piece

Stole Cross

For the stole project, make these narrow directional versions of the 3-D cross block.

FABRIC

Light: ¼ yard

Medium: ¼ yard

Dark: ¼ yard

Left-Facing Stole Cross Block

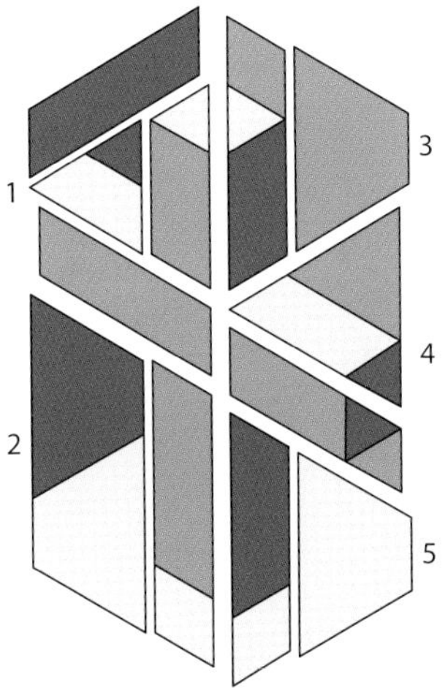

Piecing left-facing 3-D cross block

Cut these pieces for each section in the diagram.

CUTTING LIST 1

Qty & Color	Size	Shape
1 light	2″	triangle
1 dark	2″	triangle
1 light	3¼″	flat pyramid cut from a 1¾″ strip
1 medium	3″	right long diamond cut from a 1¾″ strip
1 dark	4¼″	right long diamond cut from a 1¾″ strip

CUTTING LIST 2

Qty & Color	Size	Shape
1 light	1¾″	diamond
1 light	4½″	flat pyramid cut from a 3″ strip
1 dark	4½″	flat pyramid cut from a 3″ strip
1 medium	4¼″	left long diamond cut from a 1¾″ strip
1 medium	4¼″	right long diamond cut from a 1¾″ strip

CUTTING LIST 3

Qty & Color	Size	Shape
1 light	2″	triangle
1 medium	1¾″	diamond
1 medium	4½″	flat pyramid cut from a 3″ strip
1 dark	3″	left long diamond cut from a 1¾″ strip

CUTTING LIST 4

Qty & Color	Size	Shape
1 medium	2″	triangle
2 dark	2″	triangle
1 medium	3¼″	triangle
1 light	3″	right long diamond cut from a 1¾″ strip
1 medium	3″	left long diamond cut from a 1¾″ strip

CUTTING LIST 5

Qty & Color	Size	Shape
1 light	1¾″	diamond
1 light	4½″	flat pyramid cut from a 3″ strip
1 dark	4½″	flat pyramid cut from a 1¾″ strip

1. Assemble each section according to the diagram.

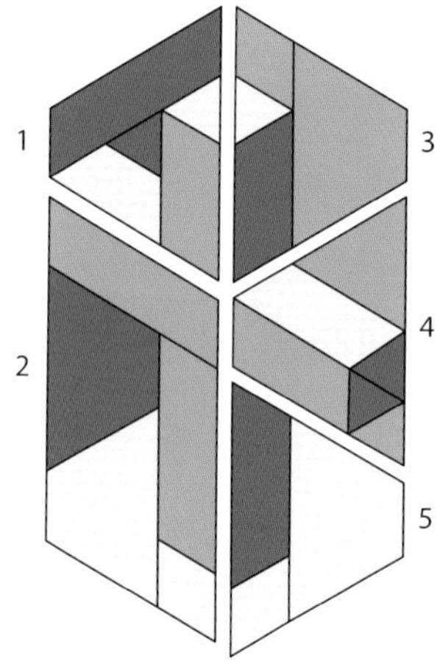

Completing left-facing stole cross block

2. Sew section 1 to section 2, making a column. Sew sections 3, 4, and 5 together as shown in the diagram. Sew the two columns together as shown to complete the left-facing stole cross block.

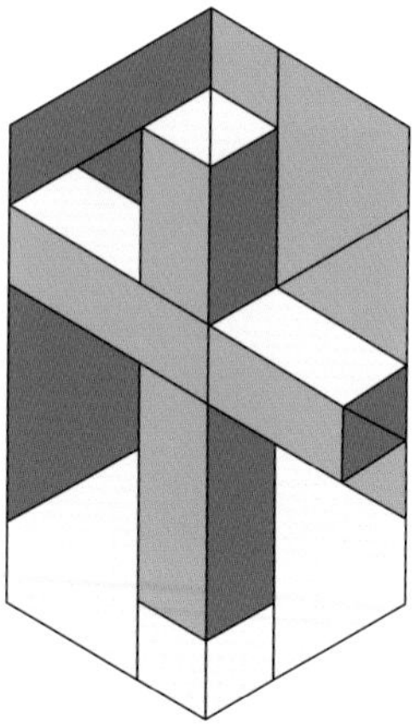

Left-facing stole cross block

Right-Facing Stole Cross Block

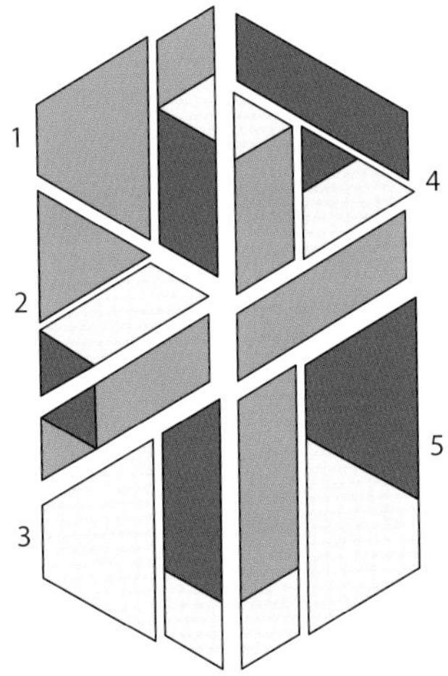

Piecing right-facing stole cross block

Cut these pieces for each section in the diagram.

CUTTING LIST 1

Qty & Color	Size	Shape
1 light	2″	triangle
1 medium	1¾″	diamond
1 medium	4½″	flat pyramid cut from a 3″ strip
1 dark	3″	right long diamond cut from a 1¾″ strip

CUTTING LIST 2

Qty & Color	Size	Shape
1 medium	2″	triangle
2 dark	2″	triangle
1 medium	3¼″	triangle
1 light	3″	left long diamond cut from a 1¾″ strip
1 medium	3″	right long diamond cut from a 1¾″ strip

CUTTING LIST 3

Qty & Color	Size	Shape
1 light	1¾″	diamond
1 light	4½″	flat pyramid cut from a 3″ strip
1 dark	4½″	flat pyramid cut from a 1¾″ strip

CUTTING LIST 4

Qty & Color	Size	Shape
1 light	2″	triangle
1 dark	2″	triangle
1 light	3¼″	flat pyramid cut from a 1¾″ strip
1 medium	3″	left long diamond cut from a 1¾″ strip
1 dark	4¼″	left long diamond cut from a 1¾″ strip

CUTTING LIST 5

Qty & Color	Size	Shape
1 light	1¾″	diamond
1 light	4½″	flat pyramid cut from a 3″ strip
1 dark	4½″	flat pyramid cut from a 3″ strip
1 medium	4¼″	left long diamond cut from a 1¾″ strip
1 medium	4¼″	right long diamonds cut from a 1¾″ strip

1. Assemble each section according to the diagram.

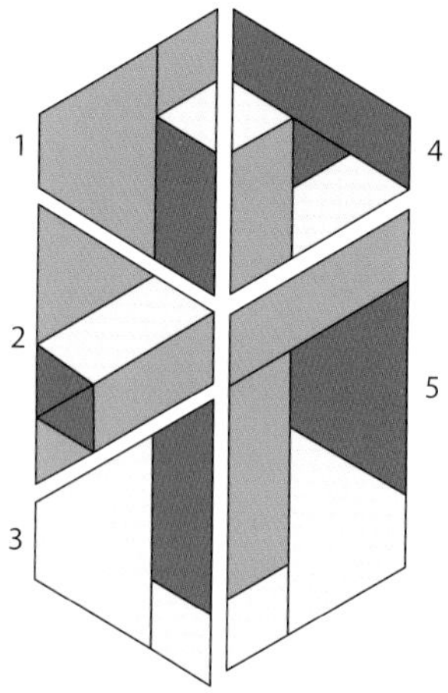

Complete the right-facing stole cross block

2. Sew sections 1, 2, and 3, making a column. Sew sections 4 and 5 together as shown in the diagram. Sew the 2 columns together as shown to complete the right-facing stole cross block.

Right-facing stole cross block

Evergreen Tree Block

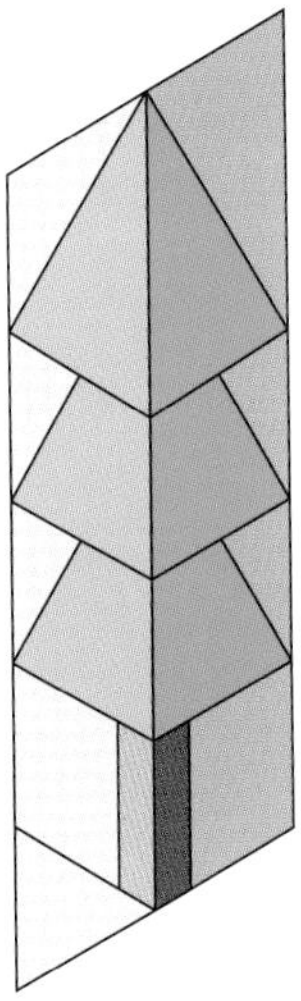

FABRIC FOR 1 BLOCK

Light sky: 3″ × 11″ scrap

Dark sky: 3″ × 10″ scrap

Light trunk: 1″ × 3″ scrap

Dark trunk: 1″ × 3″ scrap

Light leaf: 3″ × 8″ scrap

Dark leaf: 3″ × 8″ scrap

Evergreen Tree Cutting and Sewing

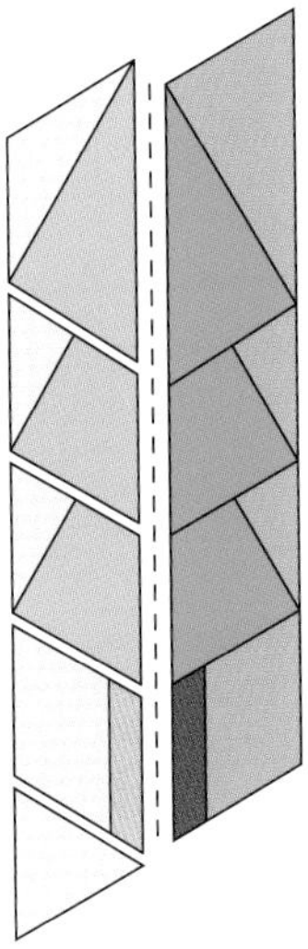

Piecing diagram

Note

This little tree is assembled in two vertical halves. The left side of the tree is lighter colored, and the right side is darker colored. Make the trunk, branches, and tips for both sides, sew the parts together in order, then sew the left and right sections together.

TRUNK CUTTING LIST

For more than 1 tree, cut sky and trunk strips in multiples of 2¼″ increments.

Qty & Color	Size	Shape
1 light sky	1½″ × 2¼″	rectangle
1 dark sky	1½″ × 2¼″	rectangle
1 light trunk	¾″ × 2¼″	rectangle
1 dark trunk	¾″ × 2¼″	rectangle
1 light sky	2″	triangle

1. Sew the light sky strip to the light trunk strip, and the dark sky strip to the dark trunk strip. Press to the sky.

2. With the trunk strip at the bottom of each strip set, cut a 1¾″ right diamond from the light strip set, and a 1¾″ left diamond from the dark strip set.

3. Sew the light 2″ triangle to the left of the light sky/trunk diamond.

TREE BRANCHES CUTTING LIST

Qty & Color	Size	Shape
2 light leaf	1¾″ × 2⅛″	rectangle; trim to 60° on *right* end to be a quarter hex
2 dark leaf	1¾″ × 2⅛″	rectangle; trim to 60° on *left* end to be a quarter hex
2 light sky	1½″ × 2½″	rectangle; cut into right triangle half from lower left to upper right
2 dark sky	1½″ × 2½″	rectangle; cut into left triangle half from lower right to upper left

1. Match the square corner of a light sky triangle to the square corner of a light leaf right quarter hexes; the tip of the sky triangle sticks out ⅝″. Sew together and trim the long ear of the triangle half after sewing. Repeat to make 2.

2. Repeat Step 1 with the dark sky triangle and the dark leaf left quarter hexes. Make 2.

Tree Assembly

As you assemble this tree, try finger-pressing and a little pinning if necessary. Not only did I find the seams butting up better, but I also felt I was making trees with my own hands; very satisfying.

TREE TIPS CUTTING LIST

Qty & Color	Size	Shape
1 dark sky	2¼″ × 3¾″	rectangle; cut into left triangle half from lower right to upper left
1 dark leaf	2¼″ × 3¾″	rectangle; cut into left triangle half from lower right to upper left
1 light leaf	2¼″ × 3¾″	rectangle; cut into right triangle half from lower left to upper right
1 light sky	1¼″	diamond half

CUTTING DIAMOND HALF

When you cut the 1¼″ diamond half, be sure to place the ruler line completely on the edge of the fabric, so that you don't cut this piece too skinny.

METHOD 1

Use the wide end of the Super 60 to cut wide triangles from the strip width given in the pattern.

METHOD 2

Place the center line of the 60° triangle on the edge of the fabric strip and cut the 30° angle. Turn the ruler over and place the center line on the edge of the fabric strip and lower corner of the ruler aligned with the previous cut edge. Cut the other 30° angle.

Make the Block

1. Sew the dark tree tip and dark sky together, lining up seam allowances for exact points. Sew the light tree tip and light sky together, matching the top points of the triangle half and the diamond half.

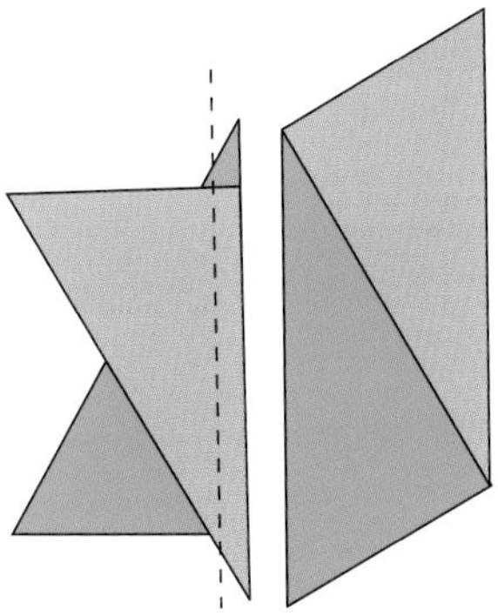

Dark tips with dog ears trimmed off

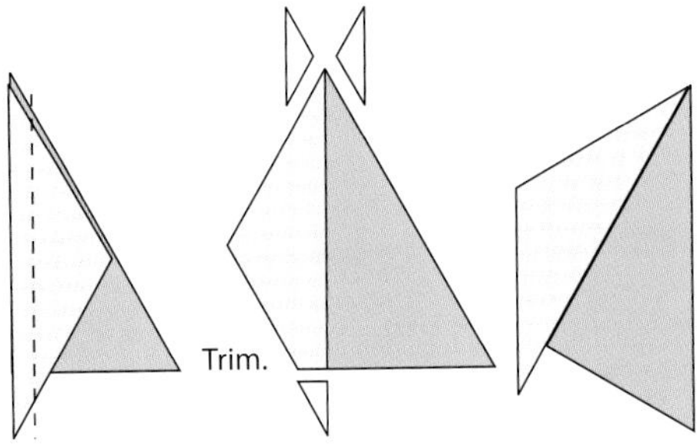

Light tips with dog ears trimmed off

2. Sew the light and dark tree tips on to the light and dark vertical sections as shown in the diagram.

3. Sew the light and dark sides of the trees together, butting the seams at the top tips. Trim the long ears at the top after sewing.

Seaming Small Pieces

Butt the center seam of the treetop, finger-pressing the seams and pin as needed. With practice, your fingertips can feel through the fabric when seams are butted up against each other. Take a peek and line it up again, pinning if necessary. The cutting angles and the small pieces go together with careful attention. Pressing the shapes under a damp cloth will flatten the fabric. Also, when the tree block is seamed in position next to the church block, it will be pulled more into correct alignment.

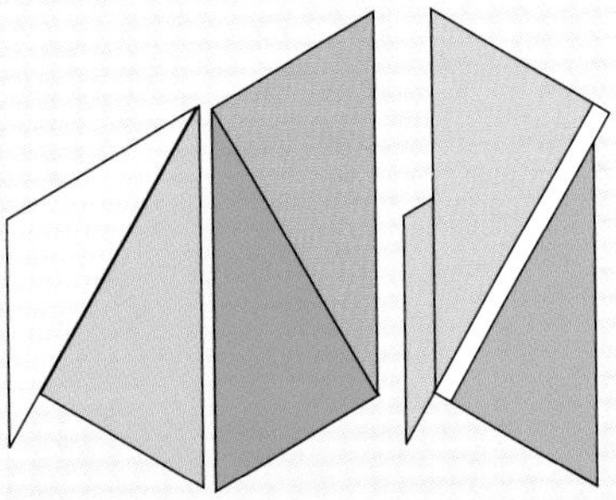

Butting tips of tree tops

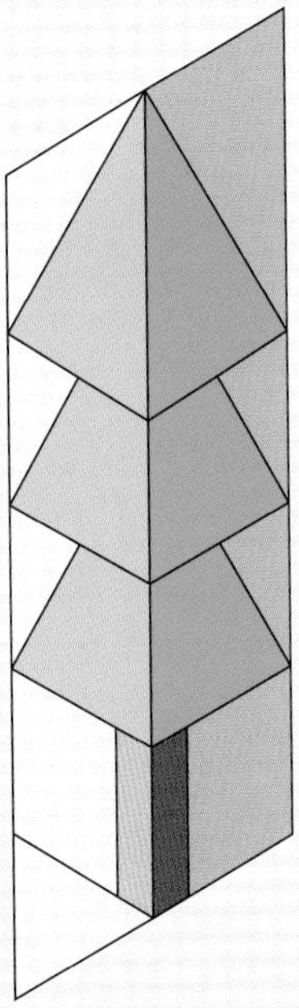

Evergreen tree

Church Block

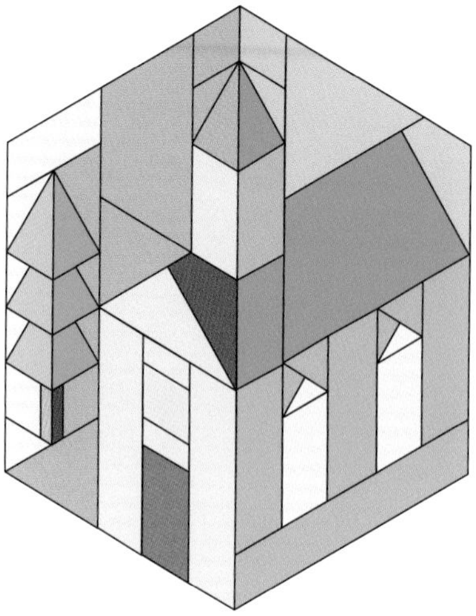

Prep the Evergreen Tree

EVERGREEN TREE EXTENSION CUTTING LIST

Qty & Color	Size	Shape
1 medium sky	3″	right long diamond cut from a 1¾″ strip
1 ground	3¼″	triangle

The evergreen tree block is part of the complete church block. Cut the above pieces to add to the tree block. Add the long diamond to the top of the tree and the triangle to the bottom to lengthen the tree for the church block.

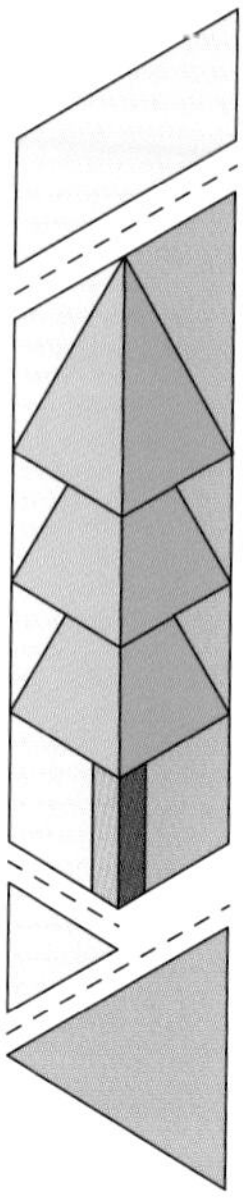

FABRIC

Light church: ⅛ yard
Dark church: ⅛ yard
Light roof: 3″ × 4″ scrap
Dark roof: ⅛ yard
Light Sky: ¼ yard
Medium Sky: ⅛ yard
Window: ⅛ yard
Door: 2″ × 5″ scrap
Ground: 4″ × 4″ scrap

Construction Tips

Since the tree contains so many pieces cut at various angles, pressing techniques may stretch or distort the shapes. A light touch can be helpful. When you sew the tree to the front of the church, start at the bottom. When you get to the top, you may need to trim the top sky strip slightly to match the 5¾″ sky flat pyramid next to it. Be sure to preserve all ¼″ seam allowances around the tree.

Piecing Left Half-block

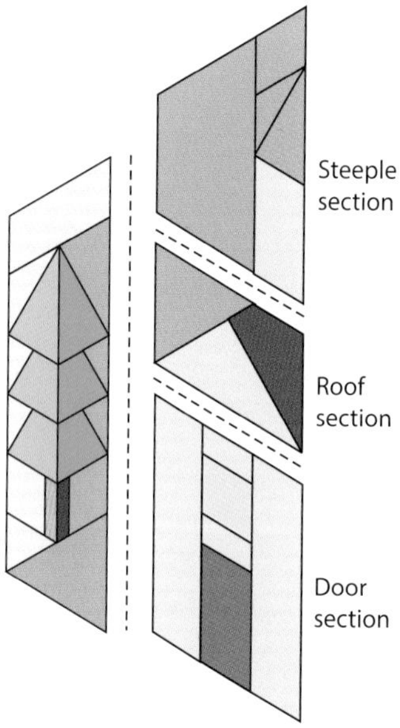

Assembly for steeple, front roof, and door

STEEPLE CUTTING LIST

Qty & Color	Size	Shape
1 medium sky	1¾″	diamond
1 medium sky	1¼″	diamond half
1 medium sky	5¾″	flat pyramid cut from a 3″ strip
1 light church	3″	right long diamond cut from a 1¾″ strip
1 light roof	2¼″ × 3¾″	rectangle; cut into right triangle half from lower left to upper right

1. Assemble according to the diagram.

ROOF CUTTING LIST

Qty & Color	Size	Shape
1 medium sky	3¼″	triangle
1 dark roof	2⅞″ × 5″	rectangle; cut into left triangle half from lower right to upper left
1 light church	2⅞″ × 5″	rectangle; cut into right triangle half from lower left to upper right

1. Sew the dark and light triangle halves together, then sew the 3¼″ sky triangle on the left and trim the roof triangle half even with the right side of the sky triangle according to the diagram.

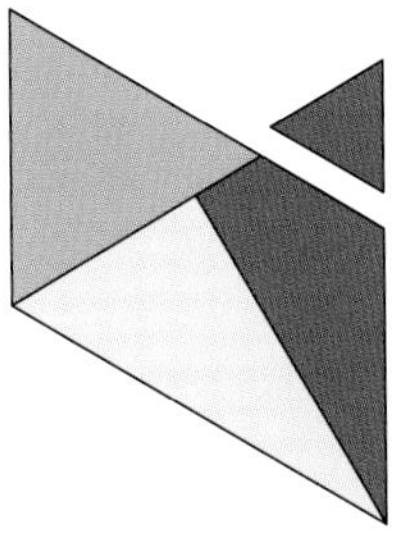

Roof assembly detail. Trim even with sky triangle.

DOOR CUTTING LIST

Qty & Color	Size	Shape
1 window	1¾″	diamond
1 door	3″	right long diamond cut from a 1¾″ strip
2 light church	1⅛″	left long diamond cut from a 1¾″ strip
2 light church	5½″	right long diamond cut from a 1¾″ strip

1. Assemble the door section according to the diagram.

2. Sew the three sections together into a vertical panel as shown. Sew the evergreen tree section on the left side to complete the Left Half-Block.

Piecing the Right Half-Block

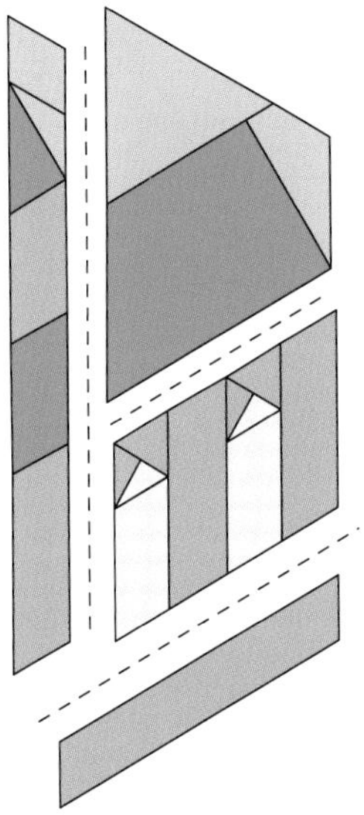

Church right half-block piecing diagram

STEEPLE CUTTING LIST

Qty & Color	Size	Shape
1 light sky	1¼″	diamond half
1 light sky	1¾″	diamond
1 dark church	3″	left long diamond cut from a 1¾″ strip
1 dark roof	3″	left long diamond cut from a 1¾″ strip
1 dark church	4¼″	left long diamond cut from a 1¾″ strip
1 dark roof	2¼″ × 3¾″	rectangle; cut into left triangle half from lower right to upper left

1. Assemble according to the diagram.

ROOF CUTTING LIST

Qty & Color	Size	Shape
1 light sky	2″	diamond half
1 light sky	4½″	triangle
1 dark roof	4¼″ × 6⅜″	rectangle cut to 60° angle on left as in diagram

1. Sew the diamond half to the right end of the trimmed rectangle with ¾″ of the diamond half extending on the bottom.

2. Trim the top even with the top of the dark roof. Nip excess off the bottom, too.

3. Sew on the light sky triangle to complete the roof section.

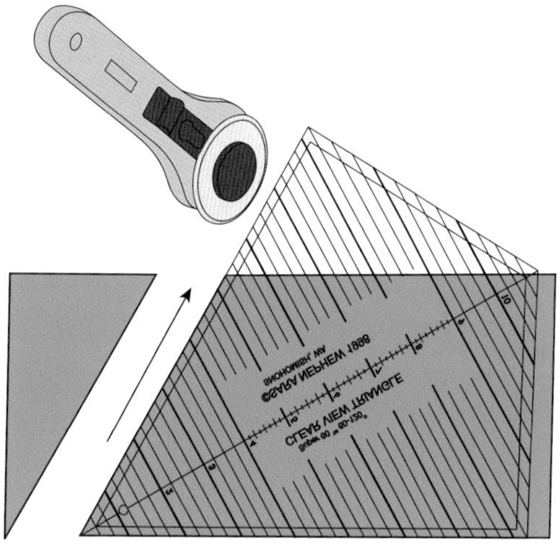

Trimming roof section

WINDOW CUTTING LIST

Qty & Color	Size	Shape
2 window	3″	left long diamond cut from a 1¾″ strip
2 dark church	4¼″	left long diamond cut from a 1¾″ strip
2 dark church	2″	triangle
2 window	1½″ × 2½″	rectangle; cut into left triangle halves from lower right to upper left
2 dark church	1½″ × 2½″	rectangle; cut into right triangle halves from lower left to upper right

1. Assemble according to the diagram.

2. Add a 6¾″ dark church right long diamond (cut from a 1¾″ strip) across the bottom of all to complete the right half-block. You now have two half-blocks that complete the church block. Do not sew the left and right half-blocks together yet.

3-D Large Cross Quilt

Finished size: 63″ × 69″

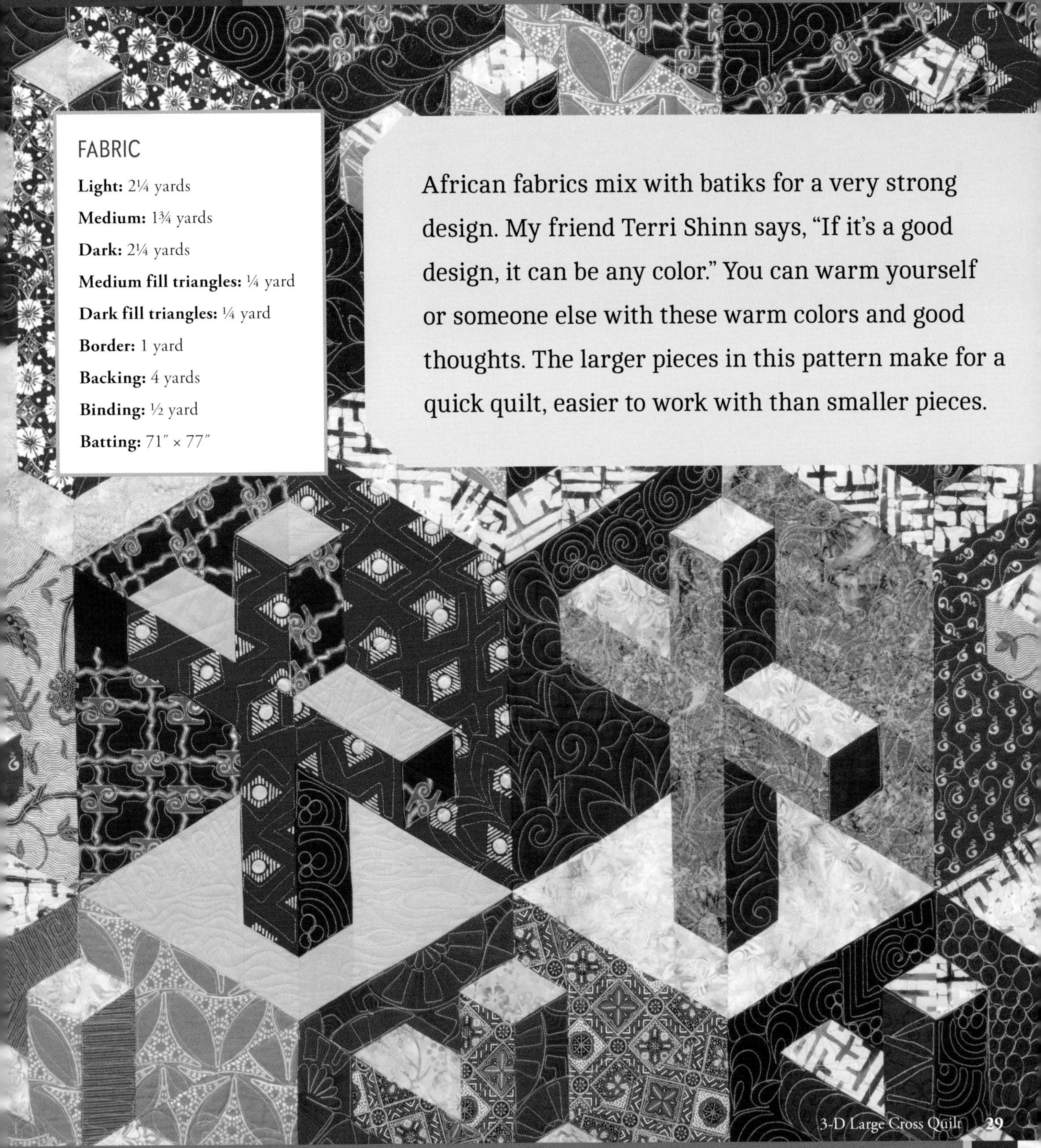

FABRIC

Light: 2¼ yards

Medium: 1¾ yards

Dark: 2¼ yards

Medium fill triangles: ¼ yard

Dark fill triangles: ¼ yard

Border: 1 yard

Backing: 4 yards

Binding: ½ yard

Batting: 71″ × 77″

African fabrics mix with batiks for a very strong design. My friend Terri Shinn says, “If it’s a good design, it can be any color.” You can warm yourself or someone else with these warm colors and good thoughts. The larger pieces in this pattern make for a quick quilt, easier to work with than smaller pieces.

Make the Quilt

1. Make 9 of the 3-D cross blocks in the larger 3″ triangle size according to the directions on page 15. Make left and right half-blocks. Do not sew the block center seam until assembling the quilt. Sew the left and right half-blocks alternately to make columns as shown in the diagram. If you are using varied fabrics, pay attention to matching the left and right half-blocks.

2. Add a triangle half to the top and bottom of each column with a triangle half cut from a 6″ × 10¼″ rectangle.

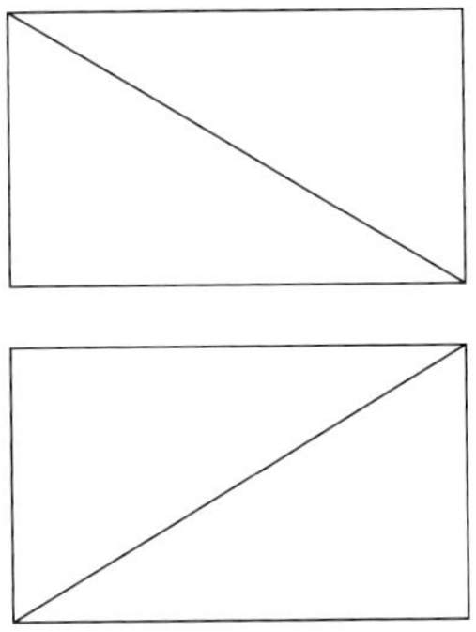

Left and right triangle halves, 6″ × 10¼″

Quilt assembly

3. Sew the columns together.

Finishing Each Project

These simple triangles can have a dramatic effect to complete the quilt. Create a straight edge by finishing top and bottom (or left and right rows of blocks depending on how you turn it) with a triangle half cut from a rectangle. The triangle size depends on the basic scale of the quilt. Then add a border to complete the quilt.

Add Borders

1. Cut 7 strips 4¾″ × width of fabric. Sew the strips together end-to-end and subcut into border pieces.

2 side borders: 4¾″ × 60¼″

2 top/bottom borders: 4¾″ × 63″

2. Sew the borders to the sides of the quilt top and press.

3. Sew the borders to the top and bottom of the quilt top and press.

3-D Small Cross Quilt

Finished size: 54″ × 67½″

FABRIC

Light: 3 yards
Medium: 2¼ yard
Dark: 2½ yards
Medium fill triangles: ⅛ yard
Dark fill triangles: ⅛ yard
Border: ½ yard
Backing: 3½ yards
Binding: ½ yard
Batting: 62″ × 76″

For once, I found fabric at the thrift store. It was an assortment of varied-sized pieces, some yards, and all new fabric. Medium-tone solid colors mixed well with large prints of lighter florals. It made me wonder if these pieces were leftovers from a successful project, or if it was an "I give up!" moment. But I do sometimes go through my fabric and find something boring that I am no longer interested in; into the bag and off to the thrift store! Even though I have shelves and shoeboxes piled with pieces of cotton, finding new prints can inspire happy sewing, so it's still worth shopping at your favorite spots.

Make the Quilt

1. Make 30 of the 3-D cross blocks in the smaller 2″ triangle size according to the directions on page 15. Make left and right half-blocks. Do not sew the halves together until assembling the quilt. Sew the left and right half-blocks alternately to make columns as shown in the diagram. If you are using varied fabrics, pay attention to matching the left and right half-blocks.

2. Add a triangle half to the top and bottom of each column with a triangle half cut from a 4″ × 6½″ rectangle.

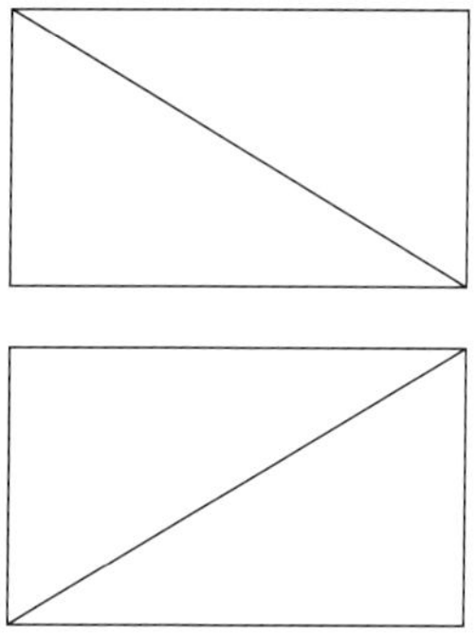

Left and right triangle halves, 4″ × 6½″

3. Sew the columns together.

Quilt assembly

Add Borders

1. Cut 6 strips 2¼″ × width of fabric. Sew the strips together end-to-end and subcut into border pieces.

2 side borders: 2¼″ × 64″

2 top/bottom borders: 2¼″ × 54″

2. Sew the borders to the sides of the quilt top and press.

3. Sew the borders to the top and bottom of the quilt top and press.

Framed Cross Quilt

Finished size: 58″ × 73″

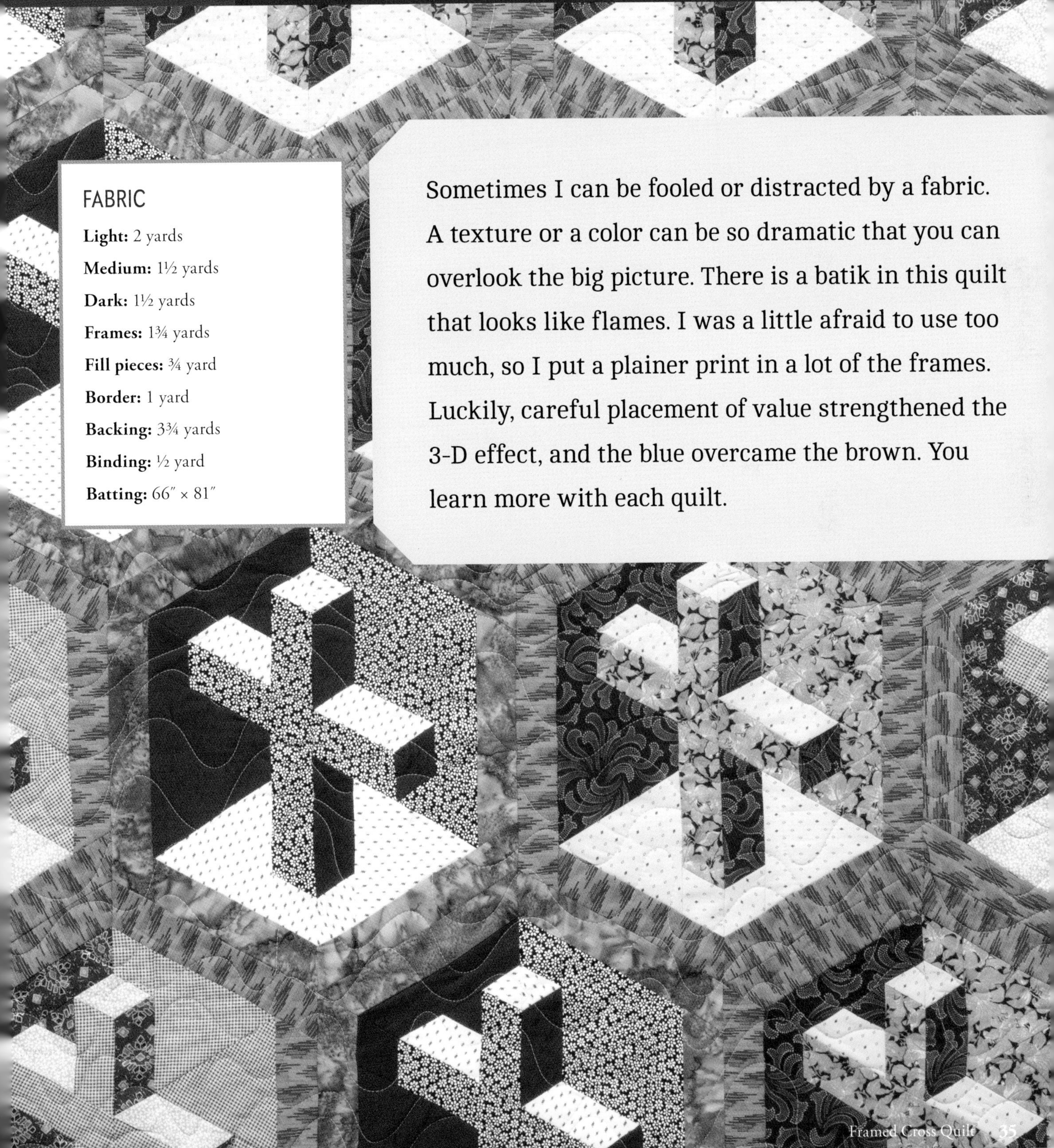

FABRIC

Light: 2 yards
Medium: 1½ yards
Dark: 1½ yards
Frames: 1¾ yards
Fill pieces: ¾ yard
Border: 1 yard
Backing: 3¾ yards
Binding: ½ yard
Batting: 66″ × 81″

Sometimes I can be fooled or distracted by a fabric. A texture or a color can be so dramatic that you can overlook the big picture. There is a batik in this quilt that looks like flames. I was a little afraid to use too much, so I put a plainer print in a lot of the frames. Luckily, careful placement of value strengthened the 3-D effect, and the blue overcame the brown. You learn more with each quilt.

Make the Quilt

1. Make 18 of the 3-D cross blocks in the smaller 2″ triangle size according to the directions on page 15. Make left and right half-blocks. Follow the instructions on page 18 to add the frame to each half-block. Do not sew the block's center vertical seam. Sew the left and right half-blocks alternately into 6 columns as shown in the diagram. If you are using varied fabrics, pay attention to matching the left and right half-blocks.

2. Make a column for the left side with 3 left framed cross half-blocks and 2 framed fill-in pieces.

3. Make a column for the right side with 3 right framed cross half-blocks and 2 framed fill-in pieces.

4. Add a triangle half to the top and bottom of each column with a triangle half cut from a 4½″ × 7½″ rectangle.

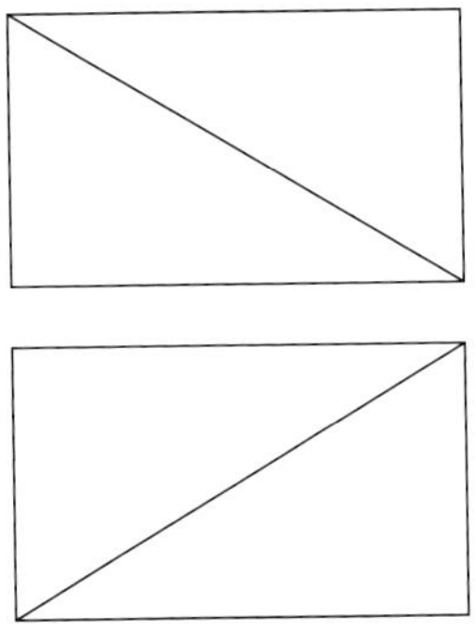

Left and right triangle halves, 4½″ × 7½″

5. Sew the 8 columns together.

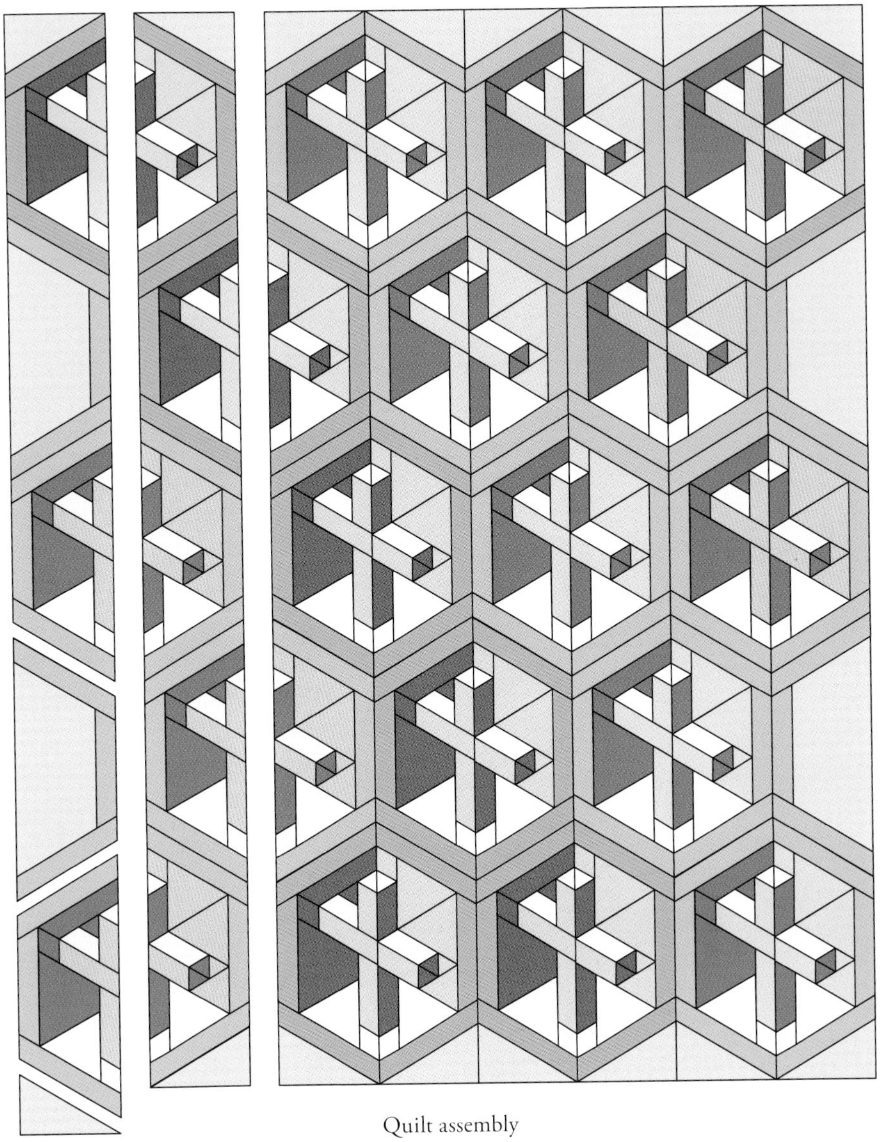

Quilt assembly

Add Borders

1. Cut 7 strips 4½″ × width of fabric. Sew the strips together end-to-end and subcut into border pieces.

2 side borders: 4½″ × 65½″

2 top/bottom borders: 4½″ × 58″

2. Sew the borders to the sides of the quilt top and press.

3. Sew the borders to the top and bottom of the quilt top and press.

Merry Christmas, Holy Christmas Quilt

(Church in the Woods Quilt)

Finished size: 47″ × 50″

FABRIC

Tree Blocks

Light sky: 3/8 yard

Dark sky: 3/8 yard

Light trunk: 1/8 yard

Dark trunk: 1/8 yard

Light leaf: 1/4 yard

Dark leaf: 1/4 yard

Church Blocks

Light church: 3/4 yard

Dark church: 3/4 yard

Light roof: 1/8 yard

Dark roof: 3/4 yard

Light sky: 1/2 yard

Medium sky: 5/8 yard

Window: 3/8 yard

Door: 1/8 yard

Ground: 1/4 yard

Other Pieces

Light fill triangles: 3/8 yard

Inner border: 1/2 yard

Outer border: 1/2 yard

Backing: 3 yards

Binding: 1/2 yard

Batting: 55″ × 58″

This quilt has two names, and I like them both. The pattern name is Church in the Woods, and seems plain and unassuming. My sister Mary said there are not enough woods. But this also happens to be my mother's maiden name: Waldkirch. Two German words—*Wald* (forest) and *Kirch* (church)—were put together into a name. So I decided to keep it as the pattern name. But then I made this quilt! I was thinking of Christmas, and I got brave with my choice of prints. I was just having fun. A metallic gold swirl on white became piles of snow and a winter sky. Snowflakes show up in sky prints, on a roof, and even in a red border. Evergreen trees swish with stripes and polka dots. And windows and wall colors glow. Put it up at Thanksgiving and enjoy it all through Christmas. It might even help you tolerate cold, gray January days.

Make the Quilt

1. Make 9 church blocks according to the directions on page 26. Do not sew the center block vertical seam. Sew the left and right half-blocks alternately into 6 columns as shown in the diagram. If you are using varied fabrics, pay attention to matching the left and right half-blocks.

2. Add a triangle half to the top and bottom of each column with a triangle half cut from a 4½″ × 7½″ rectangle.

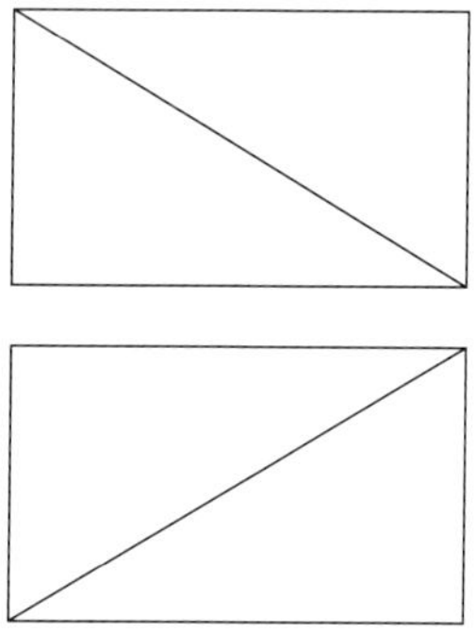

Left and right triangle halves, 4½″ × 7½″

Quilt assembly

3. Sew the 6 columns together.

Add Borders

1. For the inner border, cut 5 strips 3″ × width of fabric. Sew the strips together end-to-end and subcut into border pieces.

2 side borders: 3″ × 41″

2 top/bottom borders: 3″ × 43″

2. Sew the inner borders to the sides of the quilt top and press.

3. Sew the inner borders to the top and bottom of the quilt top and press.

4. For the outer border, cut 5 strips 2½″ × width of fabric. Sew the strips together end-to-end and subcut into border pieces.

2 side borders: 2½″ × 46″

2 top/bottom borders: 2½″ × 47″

5. Sew the outer borders to the sides of the quilt top and press.

6. Sew the outer borders to the top and bottom of the quilt top and press.

Monastery Wall Hanging

Finished size: 25¼″ × 35¼″

FABRIC

Tree Fill-in Block

Light sky: ¼ yard

Dark sky: ⅛ yard

Light trunk: 1″ × 10″ scrap

Dark trunk: 1″ × 10″ scrap

Light leaf: ⅛ yard

Dark leaf: ⅛ yard

Frame: ⅛ yard

Framed Cross Block

Light: ¼ yard

Medium: ¼ yard

Dark: ¼ yard

Frame: ⅛ yard

Church Block

Light church: ¼ yard

Dark church: ¼ yard

Light roof: 3″ × 8″ scrap

Dark roof: ¼ yard

Light sky: ¼ yard

Medium sky: ¼ yard

Window: ⅛ yard

Door: 4″ × 5″ scrap

Ground: 4″ × 8″ scrap

Other Pieces

Light fill triangles: ⅛ yard

Dark fill triangles: ⅛ yard

Border: ½ yard

Backing: 1¼ yards

Binding: ⅜ yard

Batting: 34″ × 44″

This little wall hanging could be put up instead of a crucifix—it can serve the same purpose. All you need to piece it are one and a half church blocks, a framed cross block, and a framed fill-in piece made from two evergreen tree blocks and a 5¾″ triangle. Add three triangle halves at the top and bottom to square off three columns and surround it all with a border of interesting fabric. This little quilt reminded me of a teaching trip I took to Saskatchewan. The classes were held in a monastery, and we teachers slept there, too. I remember the old buildings, mass every morning, and a bishop's cathedral not too far away. The cathedral was just a small old church, but the insides were rich with painted designs and figures.

Assemble the Blocks

- 1 church block (without the center seam sewn), page 26
- 1 left half of another church block, page 26
- 1 framed cross block, page 18
- 1 framed tree fill-in block, see below

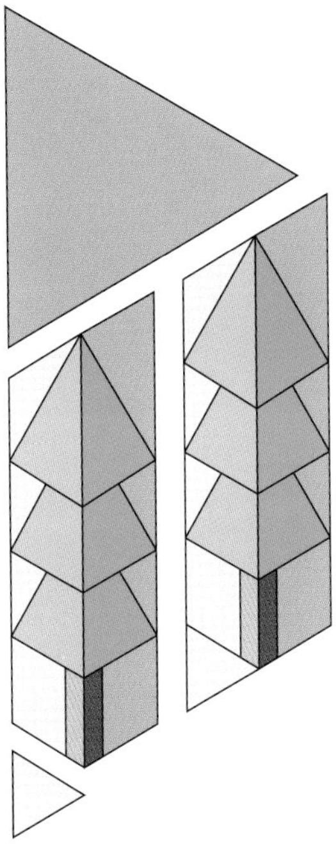

Assemble the tree fill-in block from two trees (page 23) with 2″ ground triangles and a 5¾″ medium sky triangle according to the diagram. Then frame this fill-in block as shown on page 19.

Quilt assembly

Make the Quilt

1. Sew the church block, church half-block, framed cross block, and trees fill-in block in 3 columns as shown.

2. Add a triangle half to the top and bottom of each column with a triangle half cut from a 4½″ × 7½″ rectangle.

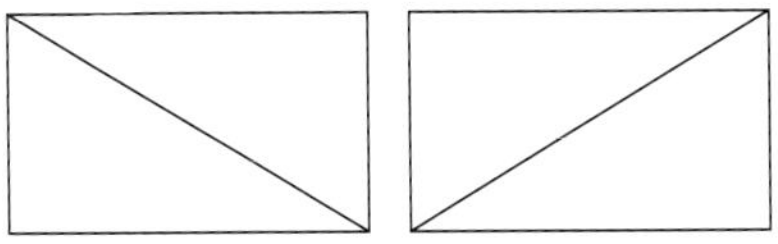

Left and right triangle halves, 4½″ × 7½″

3. Sew the 3 rows together as shown in the diagram.

Add Borders

1. Cut 4 strips 3¾″ × width of fabric, trim to size.

2 side borders: 3¾″ × 28¾″

2 top/bottom borders: 3¾″ × 24¾″

2. Sew the borders to the sides of the quilt top and press.

3. Sew the borders to the top and bottom of the quilt top and press.

Medieval Quilt

Finished size: 46½″ × 49½″

FABRIC

Tree Blocks

Light sky: ¼ yard

Dark sky: ¼ yard

Light trunk: 1″ × 13″ scrap

Dark trunk: 1″ × 13″ scrap

Light leaf: ⅛ yard

Dark leaf: ⅛ yard

Framed Cross Block

Light: ½ yard

Medium: ½ yard

Dark: ½ yard

Frame: ½ yard

Church Block

Light church: ⅜ yard

Dark church: ⅜ yard

Light roof: ⅛ yard

Dark roof: ⅜ yard

Light sky: ⅜ yard

Medium sky: ⅜ yard

Window: ¼ yard

Door: ⅛ yard

Ground: ⅛ yard

Other Pieces

Fill triangles: ⅜ yard

Border: ¾ yard

Backing: 3 yards

Binding: ½ yard

Batting: 55″ × 58″

When this project came home from the quilter, it was draped onto an overstuffed chair in the living room. For days, we looked at it. As light levels changed, we saw day and night on the crosses and churches. Sometimes the church windows glowed yellow, and at other times the temperature dropped, snow seemed to fall (in the quilt), and the scene fell more into cold blue winter evening. The depth in the picture adds meaning to a simple color scheme.

Assemble the Blocks

- 4 church blocks (without the center seam sewn), page 26
- 1 left half of a church block, page 26
- 4 framed cross blocks (without the center seam sewn), page 18
- 1 right half of a framed cross block, page 18

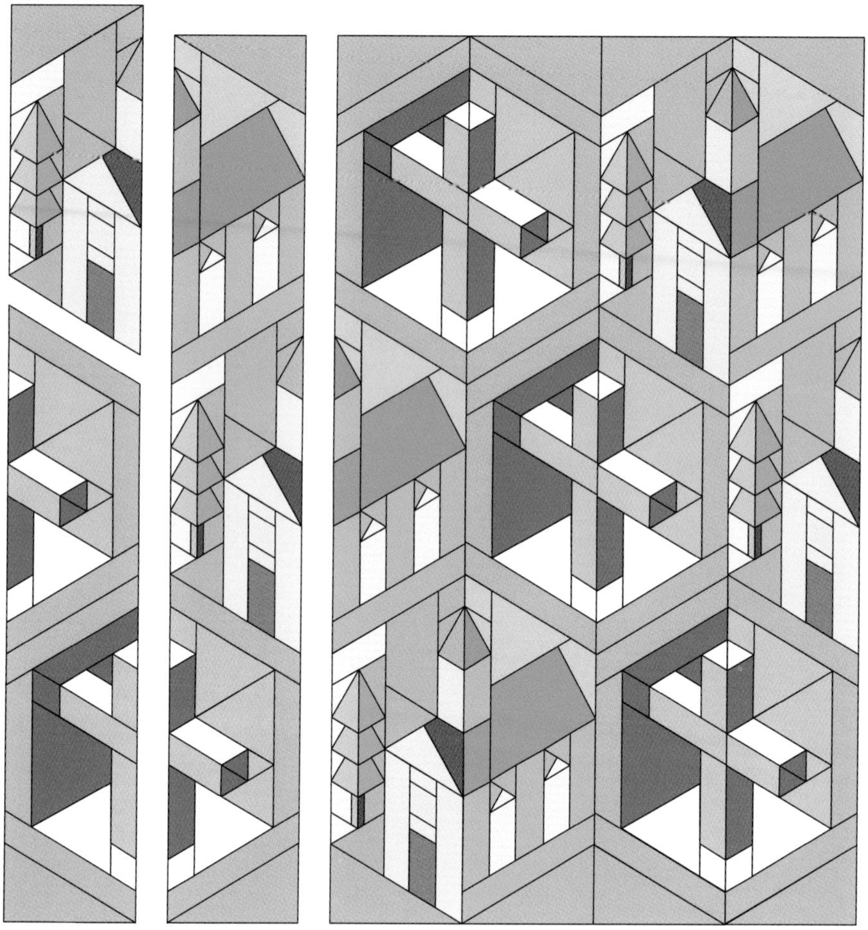

Quilt assembly

Make the Quilt

1. Arrange the blocks as shown in the diagram. Sew the left and right half-blocks alternately into 6 columns of half-blocks as shown. If you are using varied fabrics, pay extra attention to matching the left and right half-blocks.

2. Add a triangle half to the top and bottom of each column with a triangle half cut from a 4½″ × 7½″ rectangle.

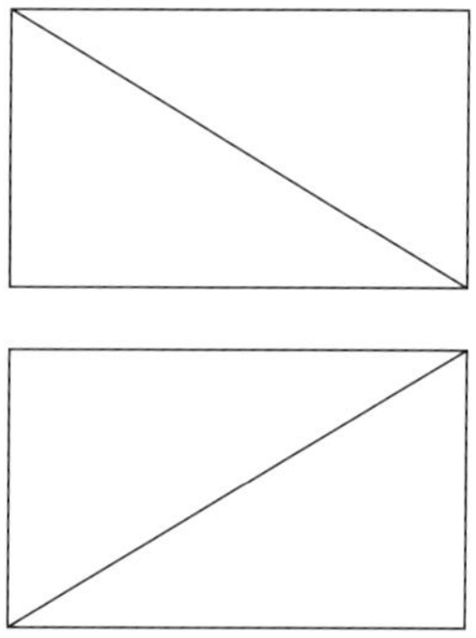

Left and right triangle halves, 4½″ × 7½″

3. Sew the 6 rows together as shown in the diagram.

Add Borders

1. Cut 5 strips 4¾″ × width of fabric. Sew the strips together end-to-end and subcut into border pieces.

2 side borders: 4¾″ × 41″

2 top/bottom borders: 4¾″ × 46½″

2. Sew the borders to the sides of the quilt top and press.

3. Sew the borders to the top and bottom of the quilt top and press.

Three Block Table Runner

Finished size: 16″ × 50½″

FABRIC

Tree Block

Light sky: 3″ × 11″ scrap

Dark sky: 3″ × 10″ scrap

Light trunk: 1″ × 2½″ scrap

Dark trunk: 1″ × 2½″ scrap

Light leaf: 3″ × 8″ scrap

Dark leaf: 3″ × 8″ scrap

Framed Cross Block

Light: ¼ yard

Medium: ¼ yard

Dark: ¼ yard

Frame: ¼ yard

Church Block

Light church: ⅛ Yard

Dark church: ⅛ Yard

Light roof: 3″ × 4″ scrap

Dark roof: ⅛ yard

Light sky: ¼ yard

Medium sky: ⅛ yard

Window: ⅛ yard

Door: 2″ × 5″ scrap

Ground: 4″ × 4″ scrap

Light fill triangles: ⅛ yard

Dark fill triangles: ⅛ yard

Fill half-hexagons: ¼ yard

Backing: 1¾ yards

Binding: ⅜ yard

Batting: 24″ × 59″

This is a simple project, but as I put the blocks together, I started seeing a variety of different clouds in the fabric. Then adding dark on the bottom of the scene helped keep the church from falling below the horizon. Scraps of dark and light binding extended the scene. I love using scraps; it's so much the essence of quilting. And there's lots of green. Do you make a green dinner on St. Patrick's Day?

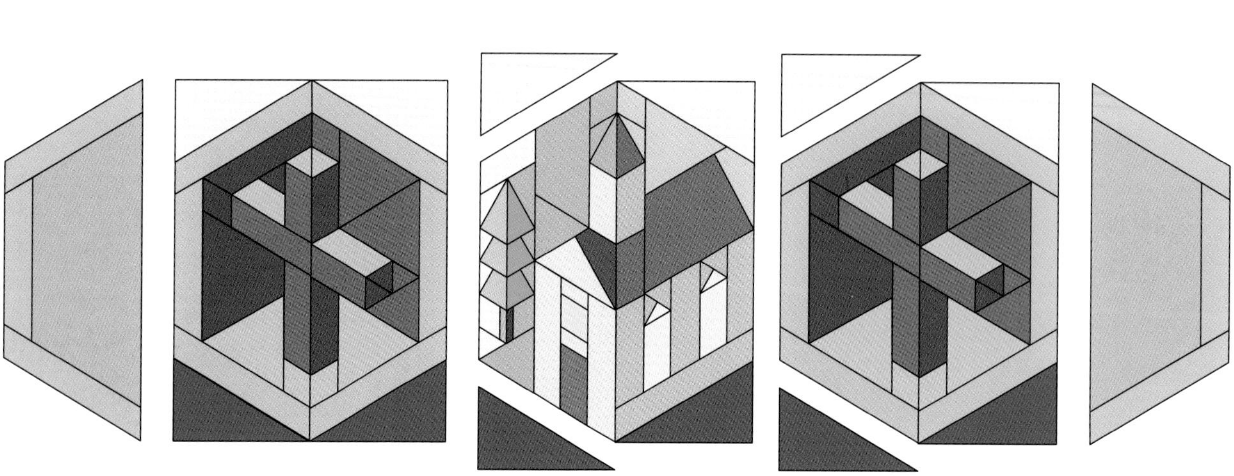

Quilt assembly

Make Quilt

1. Make 1 church block and 2 framed cross blocks.

2. Square each block off on all four corners with a triangle cut from a 4½″ × 7½″ scrap rectangle.

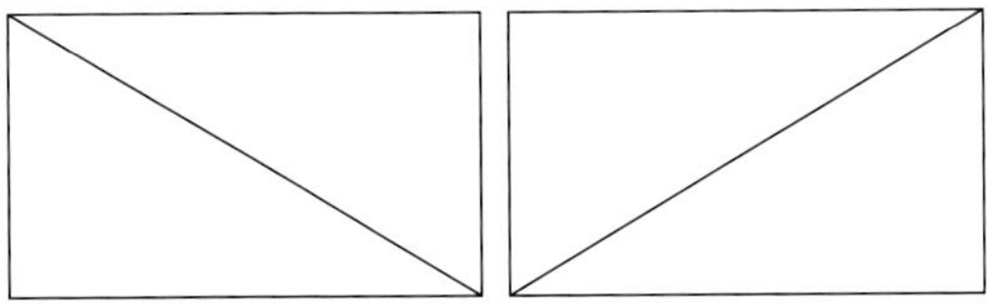

Left and right triangle halves, 4½″ × 7½″

3. Make 2 framed fill-in pieces, as shown on page 19.

4. Sew the 3 squared blocks into a row with the church block in the center. Then add a framed fill-in piece on each end.

Note

Any three blocks of the church or framed cross blocks can be used in any order, since they are the same size. Use all of one kind, or mix and match in any order, but check to see how it looks before you sew them together.

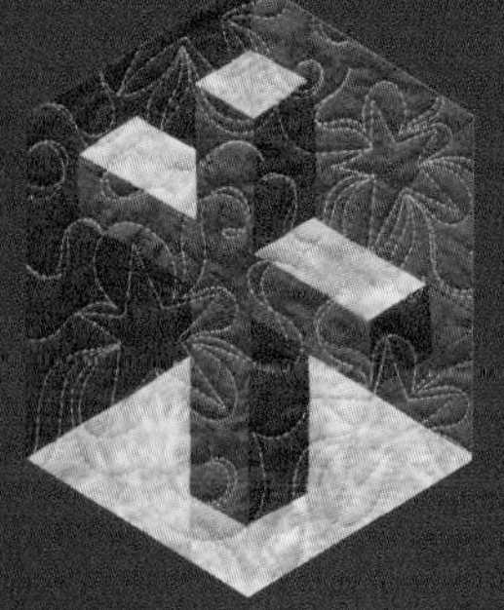

3-D Cross Banner

Finished size: 25½″ × 39¼″

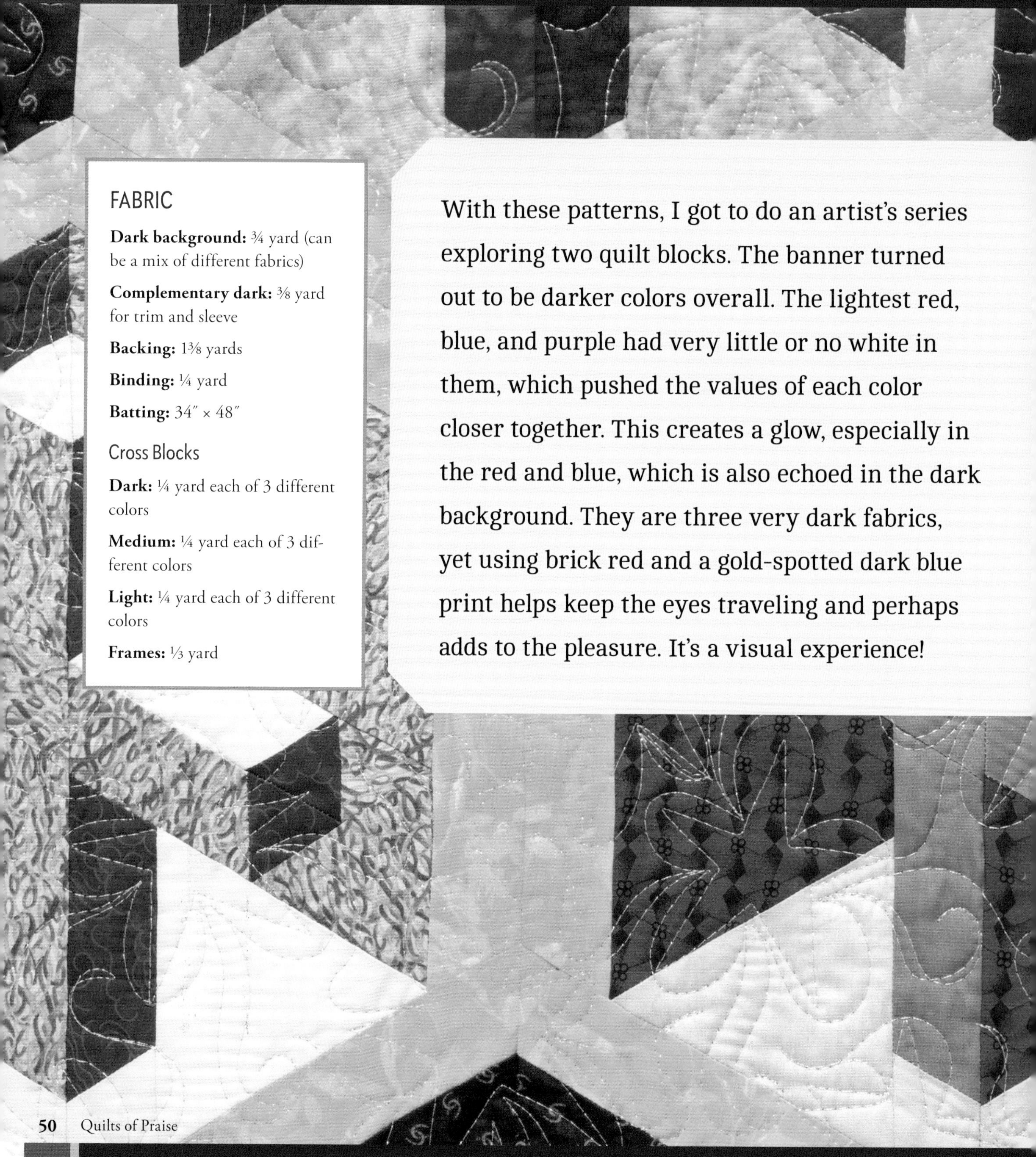

FABRIC

Dark background: ¾ yard (can be a mix of different fabrics)

Complementary dark: ⅜ yard for trim and sleeve

Backing: 1⅜ yards

Binding: ¼ yard

Batting: 34″ × 48″

Cross Blocks

Dark: ¼ yard each of 3 different colors

Medium: ¼ yard each of 3 different colors

Light: ¼ yard each of 3 different colors

Frames: ⅓ yard

With these patterns, I got to do an artist's series exploring two quilt blocks. The banner turned out to be darker colors overall. The lightest red, blue, and purple had very little or no white in them, which pushed the values of each color closer together. This creates a glow, especially in the red and blue, which is also echoed in the dark background. They are three very dark fabrics, yet using brick red and a gold-spotted dark blue print helps keep the eyes traveling and perhaps adds to the pleasure. It's a visual experience!

Make the Banner

1. Make 3 of the framed cross blocks according to the directions on page 18. Do not sew the center vertical seam of the blocks.

2. Cut 2 background 7″ × 17″ rectangles. Trim the end of one rectangle to a 60° angle. Trim the other rectangle on the opposite end so they are mirror images.

3. Add a triangle half to the top and bottom of the 2 center columns and to the bottom of the 2 outer columns, with a triangle half cut from a 4½″ × 7½″ dark background rectangle.

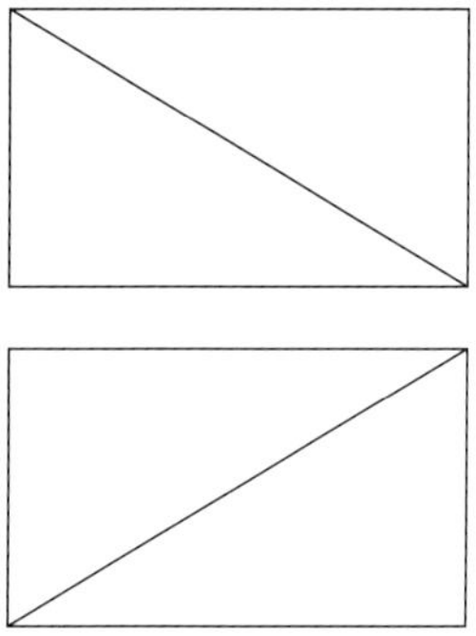

Left and right triangle halves, 4½″ × 7½″

4. Sew the 4 columns as shown in the diagram, matching the block colors.

5. For the bottom framed fill-in piece, cut a 7½″ × 22¾″ background rectangle. Trim the panel to a 60° angle at both ends, as shown in the diagram.

6. Cut a complementary dark strip 1¾″ × width of fabric. Trim one end to a 60° angle. Sew to the long bottom edge of the panel and trim the other end as shown.

7. From the remaining strip, cut a complementary 9″ dark left and right long diamond. Sew each long diamond on either side of the panel from Step 6.

8. Sew the panel to the bottom of the crosses section.

9. Cut a 3″ × 25½″ dark background rectangle. Sew to the top of the banner.

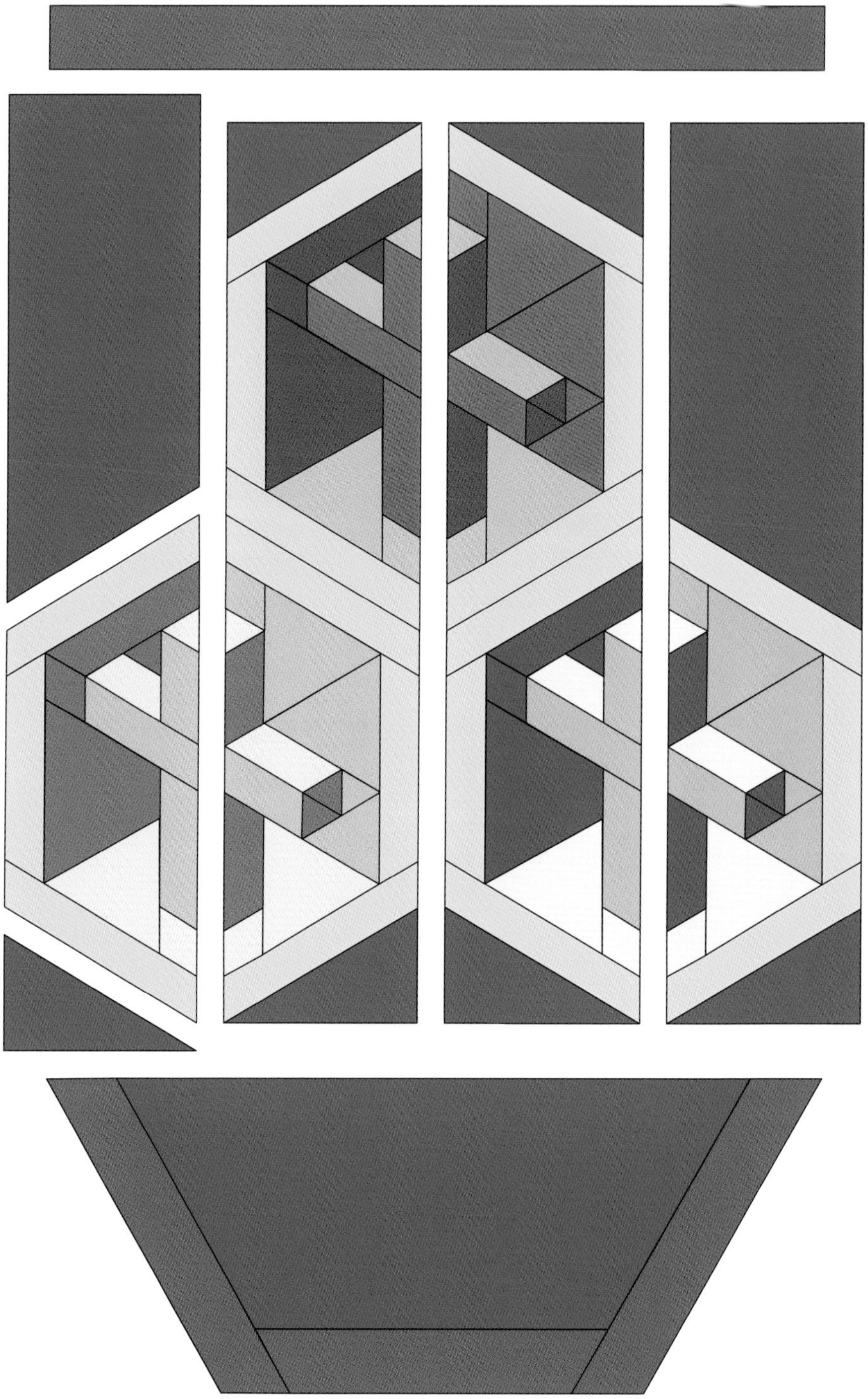

Quilt assembly

10. After the banner is quilted and bound, add a sleeve to hang the banner. Cut a 9″ × 26″ rectangle. With the wrong sides together, sew the long edges together. Press the seam open. Hem each end of the tube and sew to the top back of the banner.

Liturgical Stole

Finished size: 7½″ × 98½″

MATERIALS

Base Fabric: 1½ yards

Fusible Interfacing: 1½ yards at 20″ width (I used Shape Flex.)

Light: ¼ yard

Medium: ¼ yard

Dark: ¼ yard

¼″-wide double-sided wash away tape (optional)

This stole was a challenge for me. I saved it for last. There are lots of pictures online of different styles of liturgical garments, with different fabrics (and different prices!). There are also books on making these garments. Making a simple pattern narrowed down the choices; choosing to use cotton and then sorting through cotton prints for inspiration gave the final push. It was not as hard as I anticipated! I'm proud of myself and happy with the baptismal stole with the 3-D crosses.

I enjoyed working with cotton for this stole since it's not slippery or fragile. The blue print was a little heavier than the lining, which I think was also an advantage. I have seen antique liturgical garments made from silk and threaded with gold, and I can't help thinking of the hours and skill that went into such a garment. Another aspect to consider is the color and the print. You may need to match the color to the liturgical calendar, depending on the user. In this case, I was told blue was suitable for Advent. I also felt that the blue color and the print that looks like waves would be beautiful for a baptism.

CUT SHAPES

Paper Copy

Make a paper copy of the stole pattern. I used folded blank newsprint, using the fold to indicate the grainline. Place the copy on the base fabric and carefully cut around it. Then trim the ¼″ seam allowance off of the copy and use it to cut the interfacing pieces.

Print the pattern found by following this QR code or type the web address provided into your browser window:

tinyurl.com/11512-patterns-download

Using the full stole pattern, cut 2 stole fronts and 2 stole linings from your base fabric. Then cut 2 pieces from your fusible interfacing on the stitching line, as shown in the diagram. Transfer markings from the pattern to the stole front pieces.

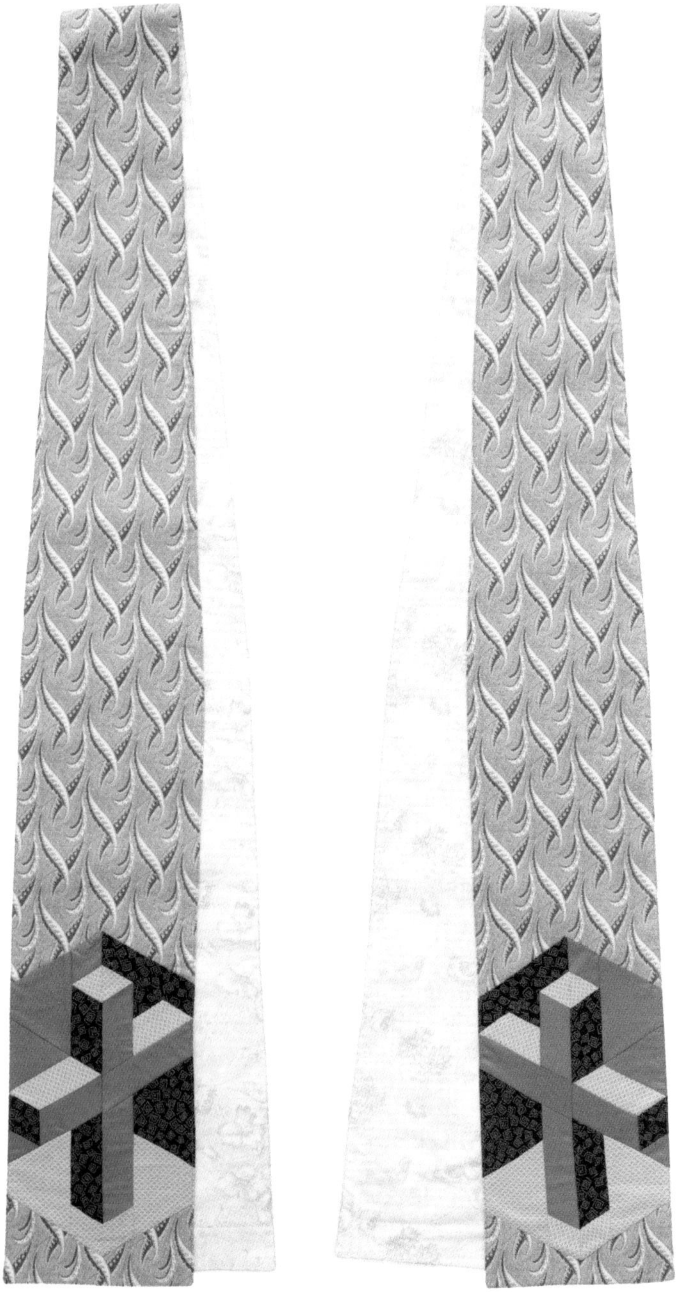

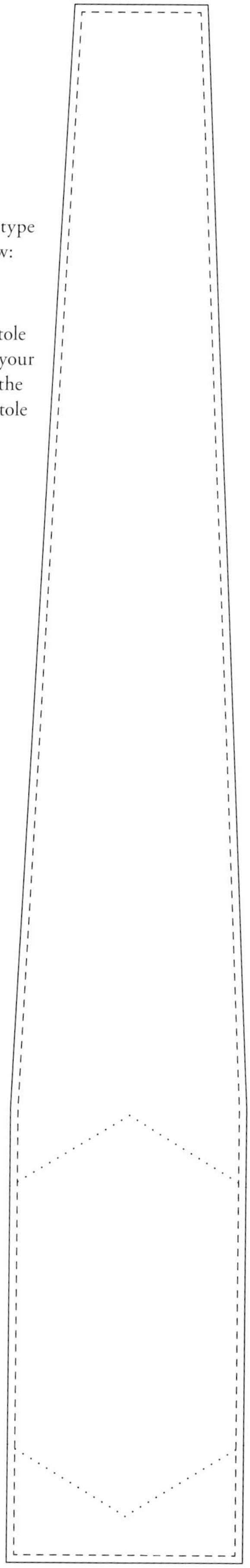

Assemble the Blocks

- 1 left-facing stole cross block, page 19
- 1 right-facing stole cross block, page 19

Piecing the Stole

1. Fuse the interfacing to the wrong side of the stole fronts. Make sure the seam allowances remain free of interfacing.

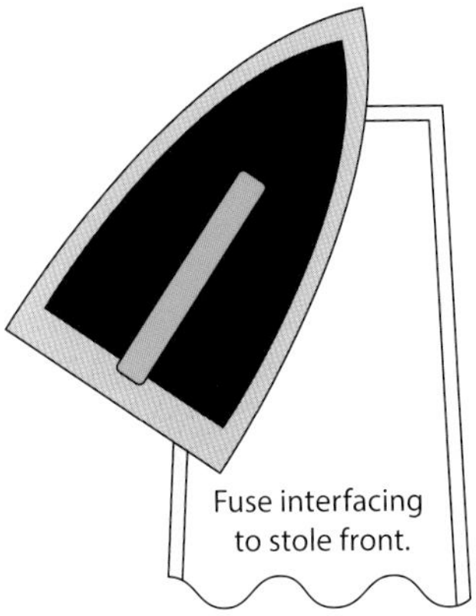

2. Press under ¼″ seam allowances on the upper and lower edges of the cross blocks.

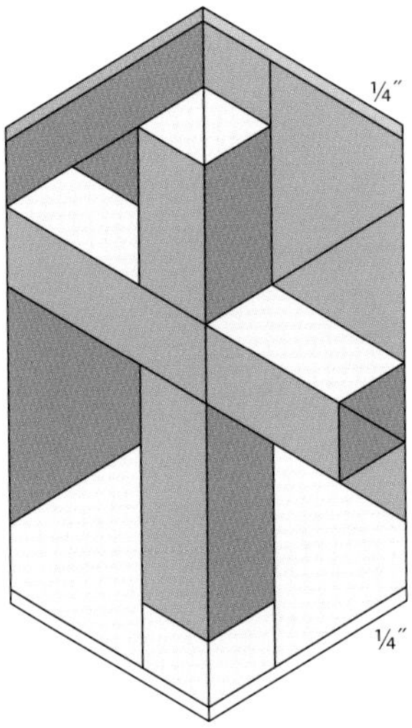

3. Place the cross blocks on stole fronts, matching the placement lines, with the raw side edges of the blocks even with the raw side edges of the stole front.

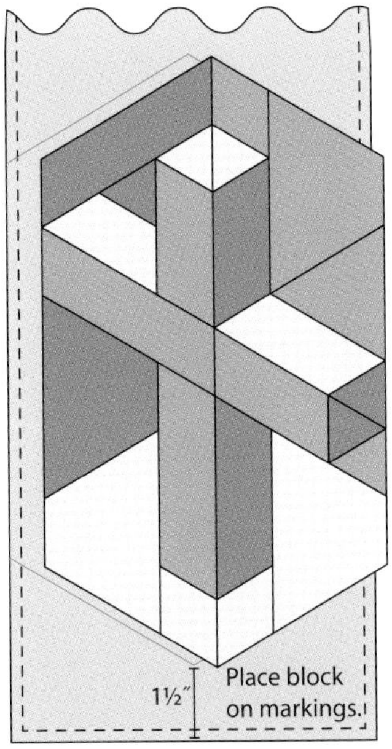

4. Using your preferred method, appliqué the blocks to the stole fronts at the upper and lower edges.

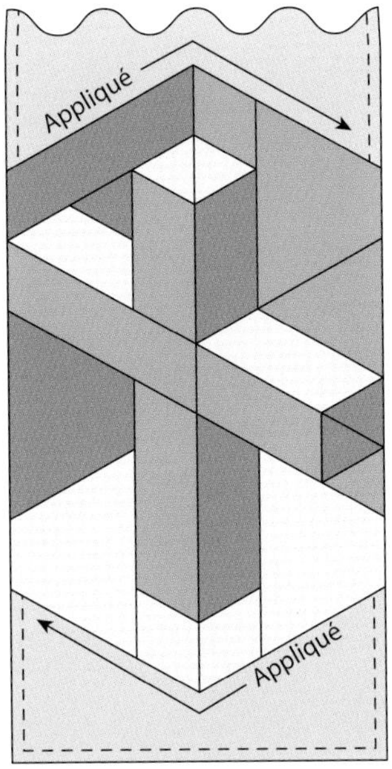

5. Sew the 2 stole fronts together at the center back. Press the seam open. Repeat for the 2 stole linings.

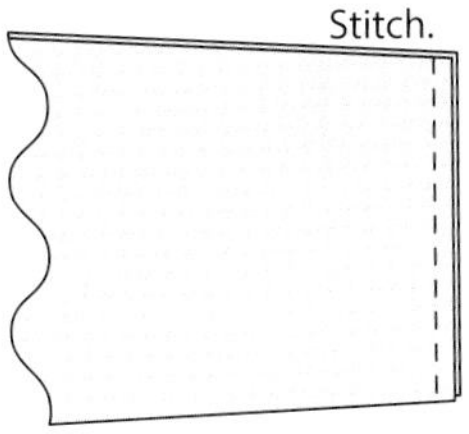

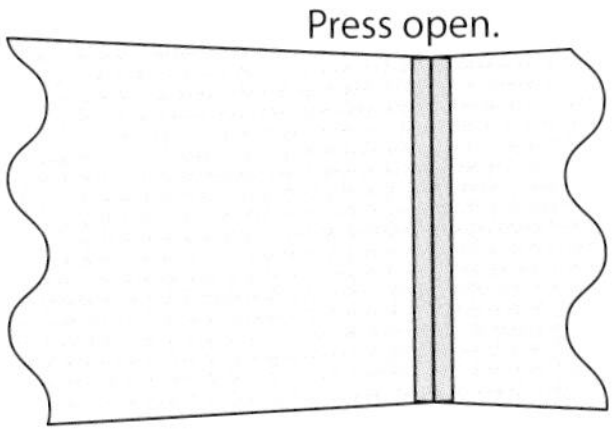

Wash Away Tape

¼″-wide double-sided wash away tape can be applied to the turned under seam allowances to help hold the block in place.

6. Place stole front and stole lining right sides together. Sew all around, leaving a 6″ opening for turning.

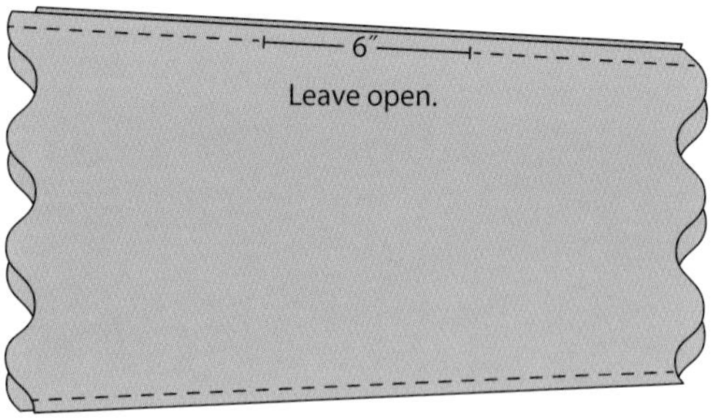

7. Clip the corners and turn the stole right side out. Push out the corners and press the seam.

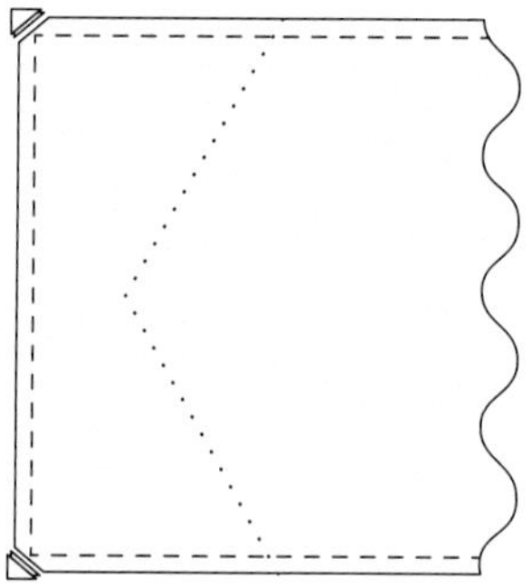

8. Edgestitch the seam to finish the stole.

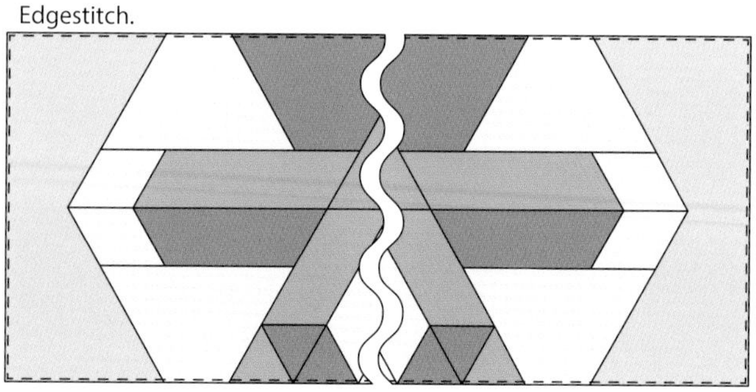

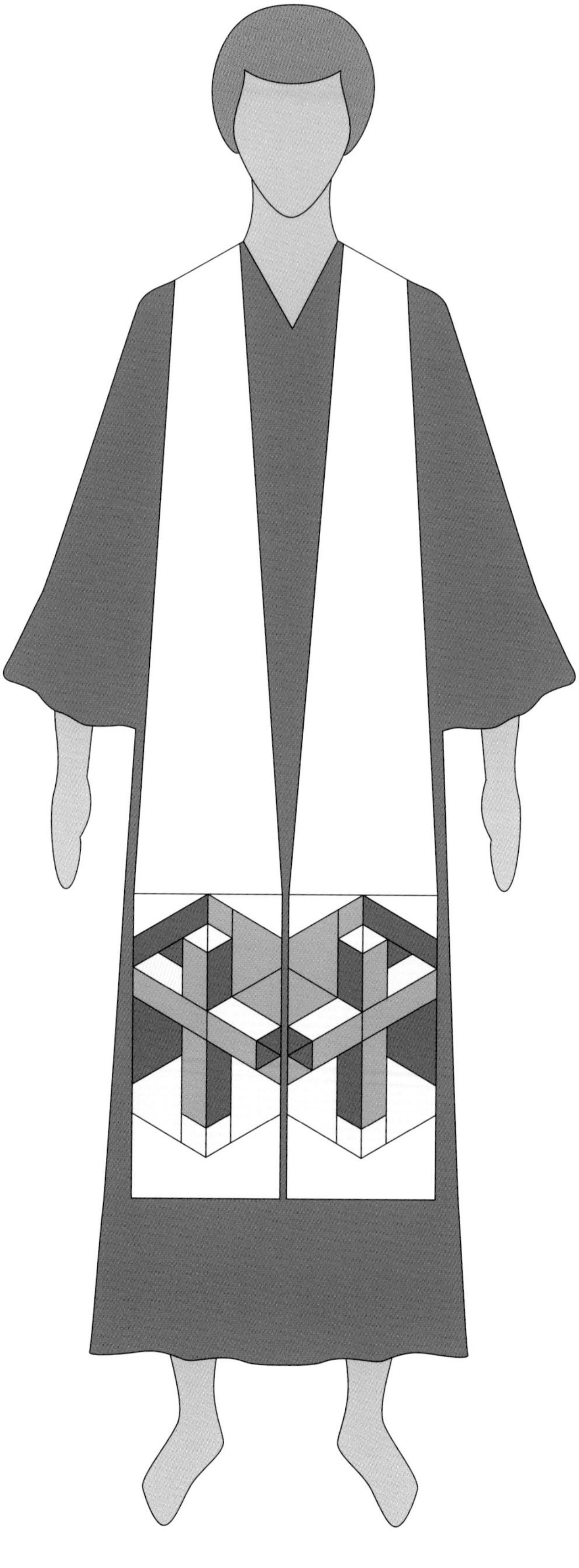

Patterns

Print all full-size templates by following this QR code or typing the web address provided into your browser window:

tinyurl.com/11512-patterns-download

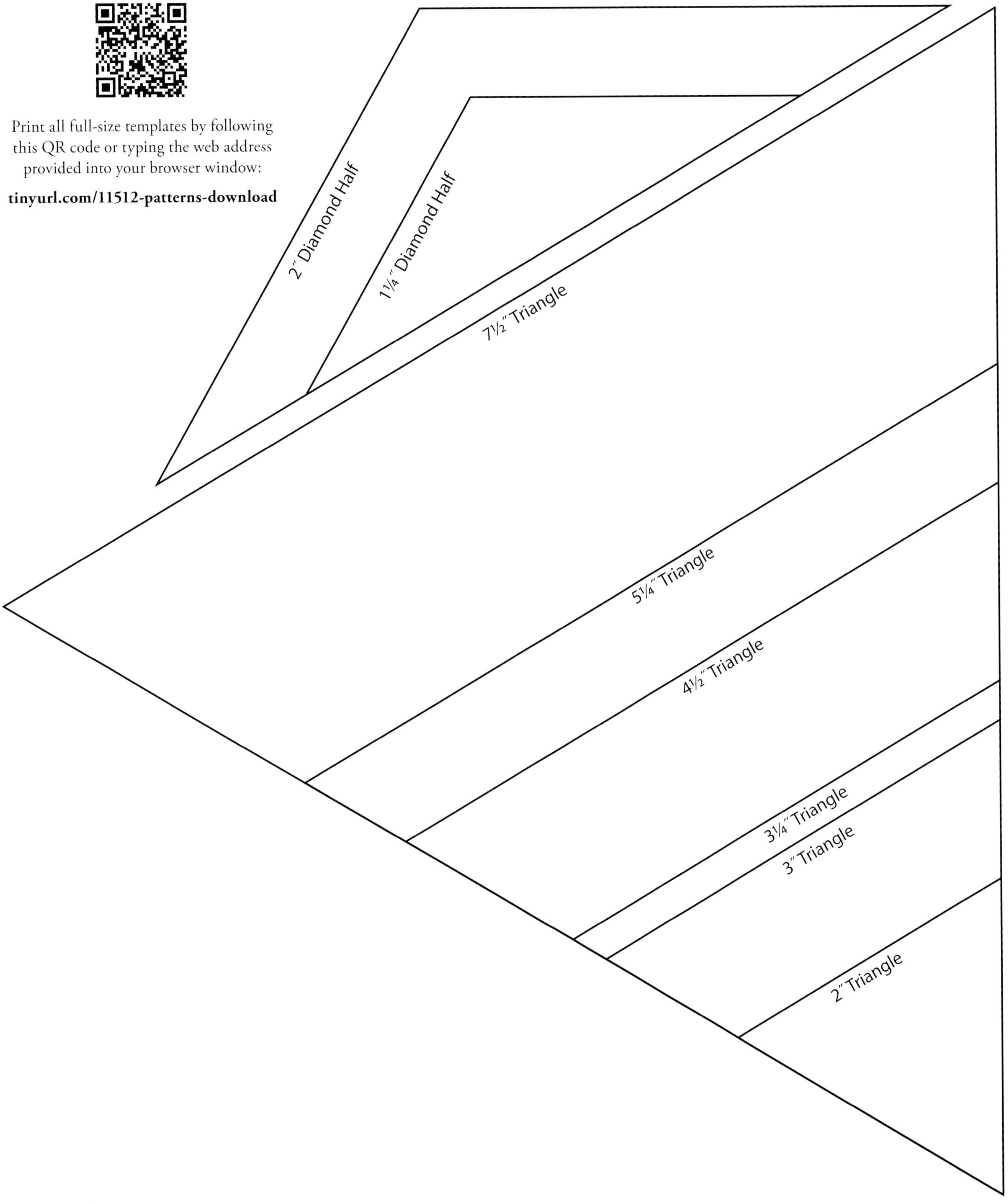

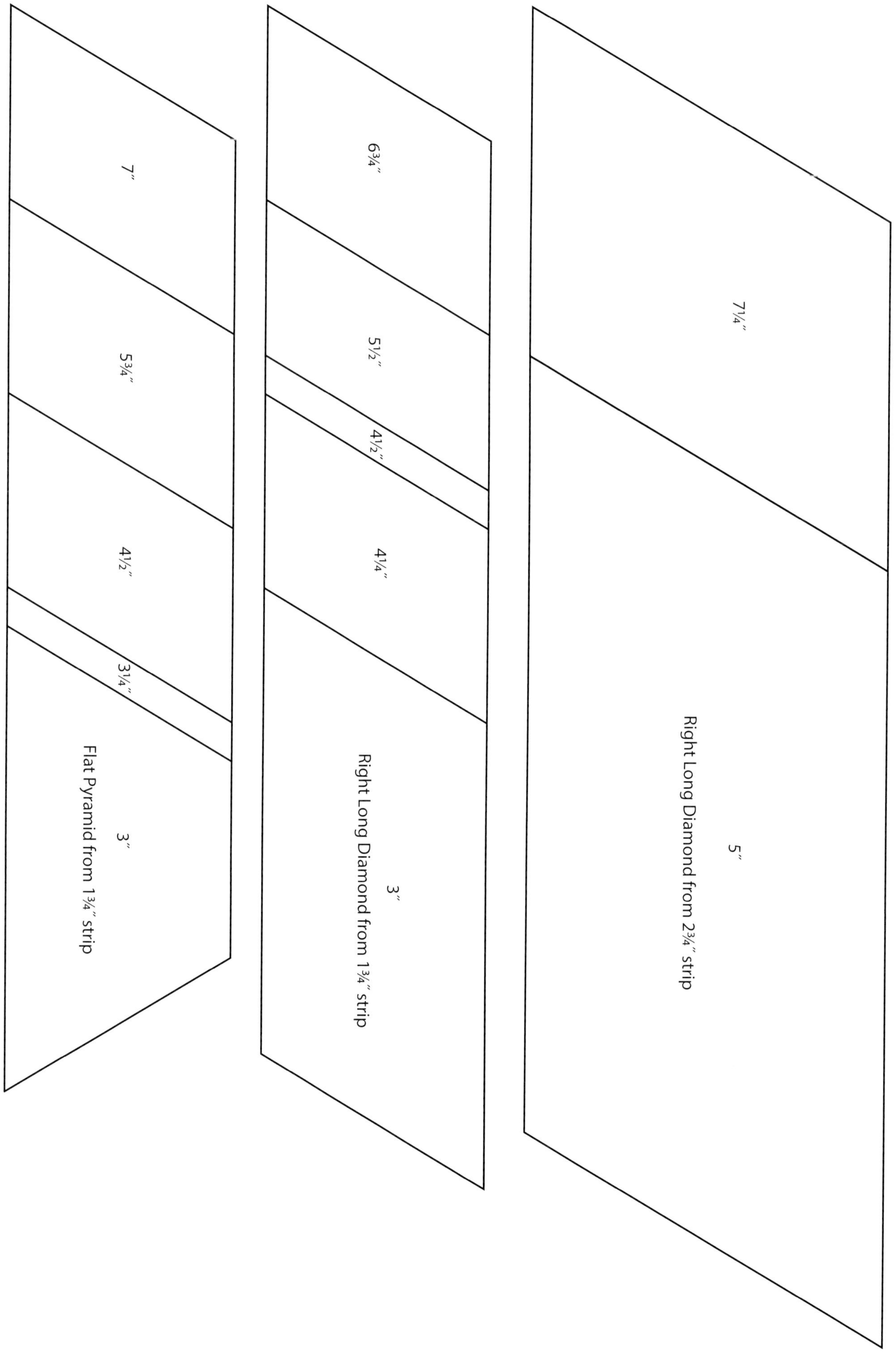
7"
5¾"
4½"
3¼"
3"
Flat Pyramid from 1¾" strip
6¾"
5½"
4½"
4¼"
3"
Right Long Diamond from 1¾" strip
7¼"
5"
Right Long Diamond from 2¾" strip

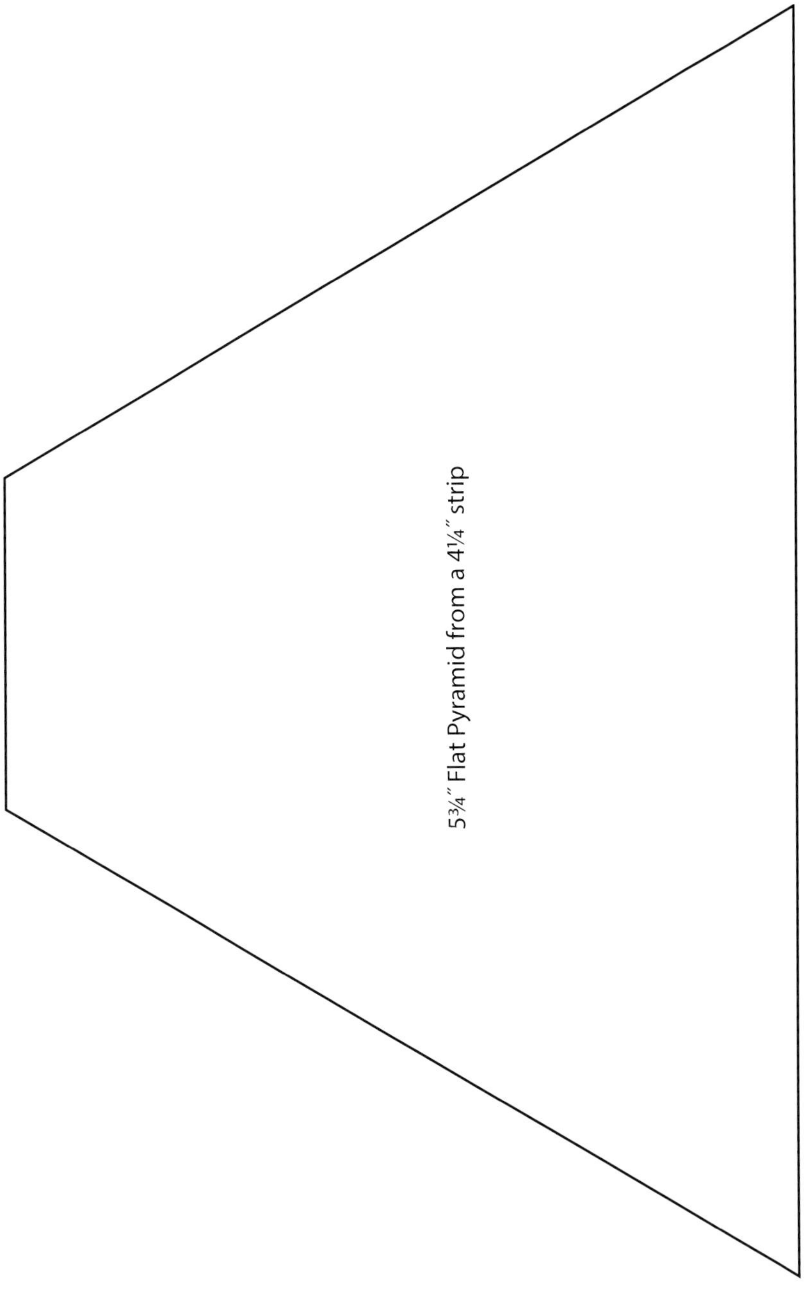
5¾″ Flat Pyramid from a 4¼″ strip

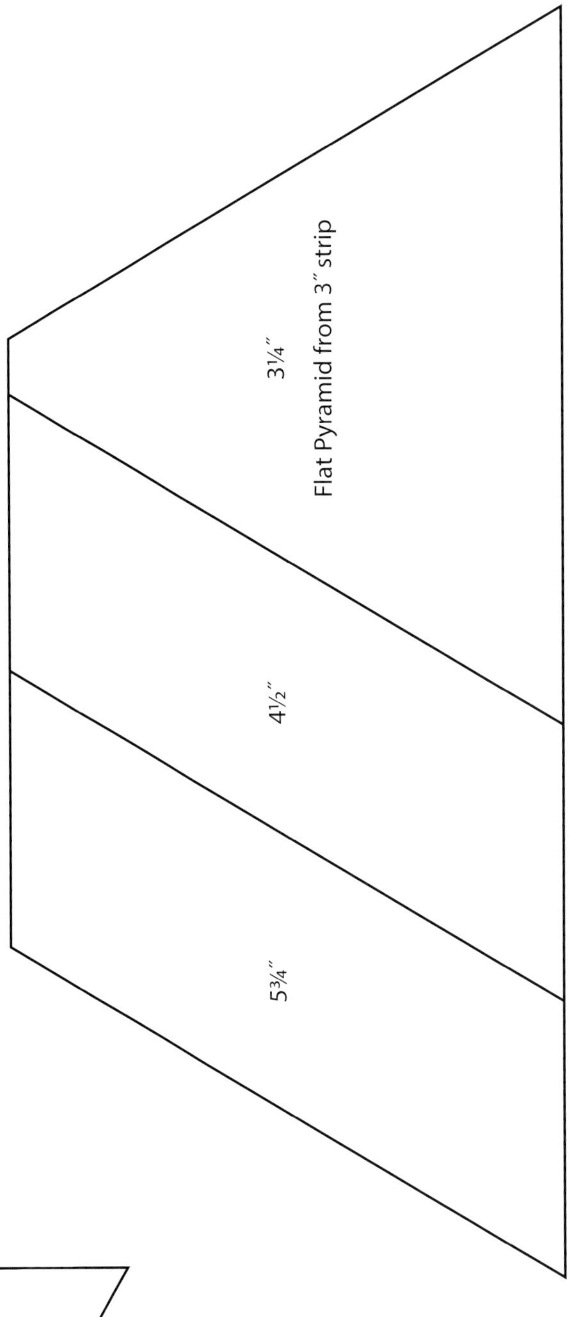
Flat Pyramid from 3″ strip
3¼″
4½″
5¾″

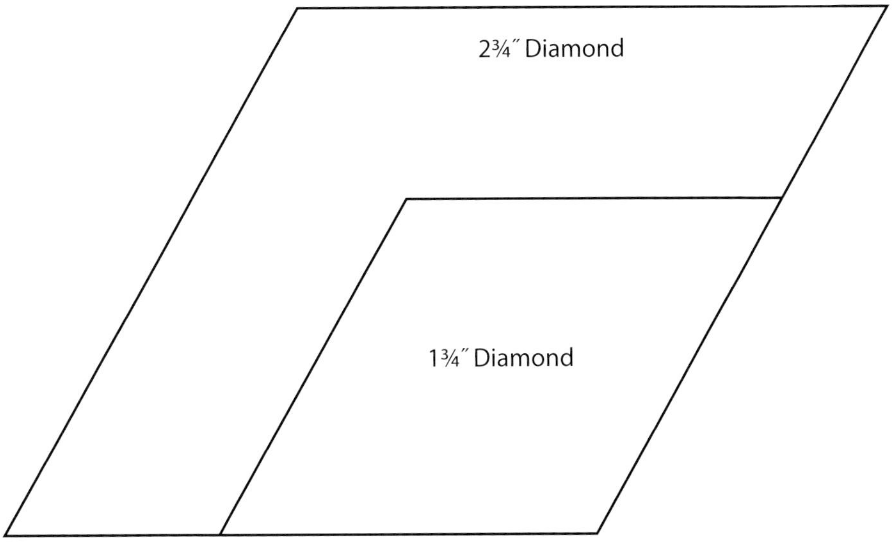
2¾″ Diamond
1¾″ Diamond

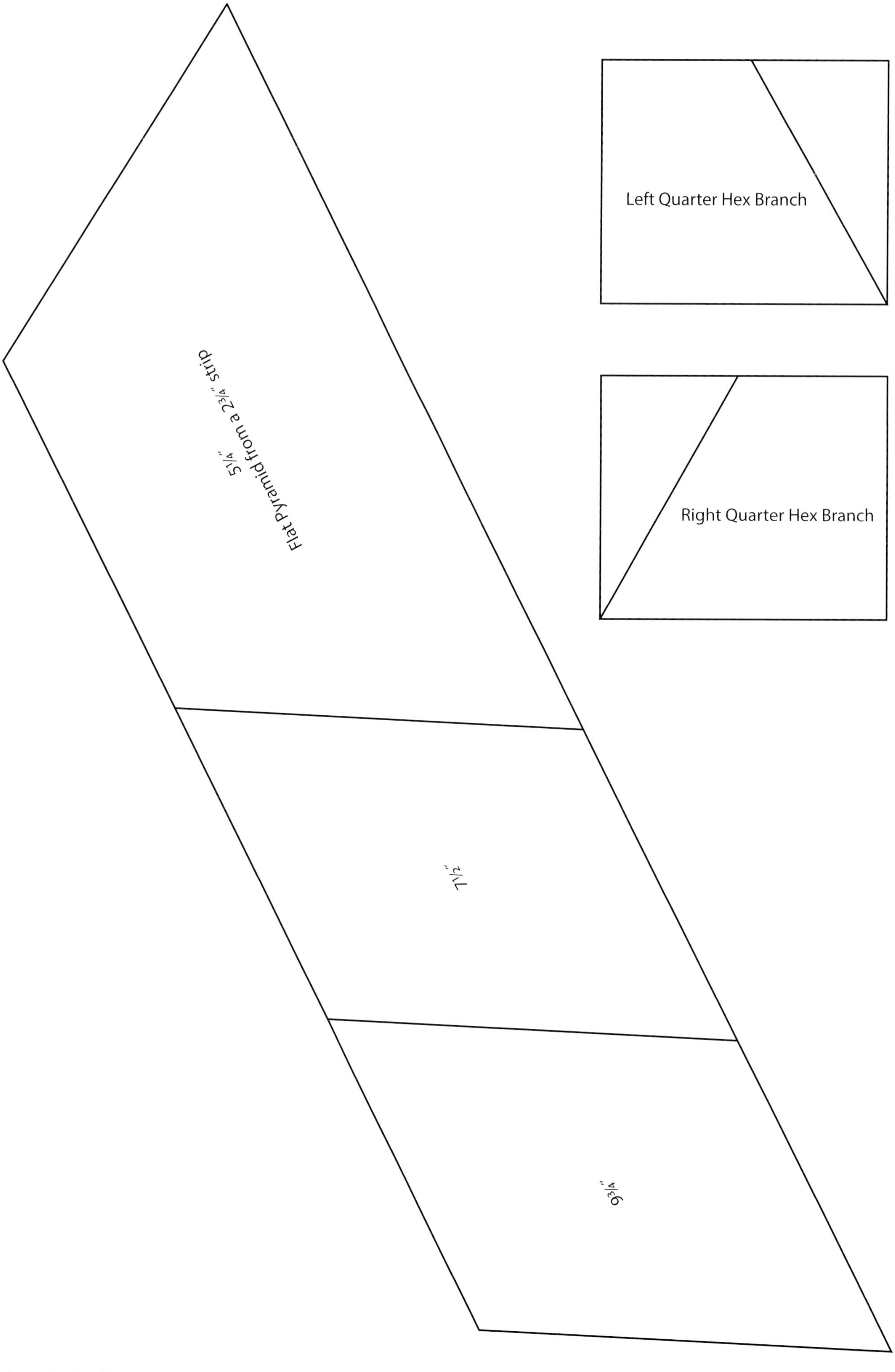
Left Quarter Hex Branch
Right Quarter Hex Branch
Flat Pyramid from a 2¾" strip
5¼"
7½"
9¾"

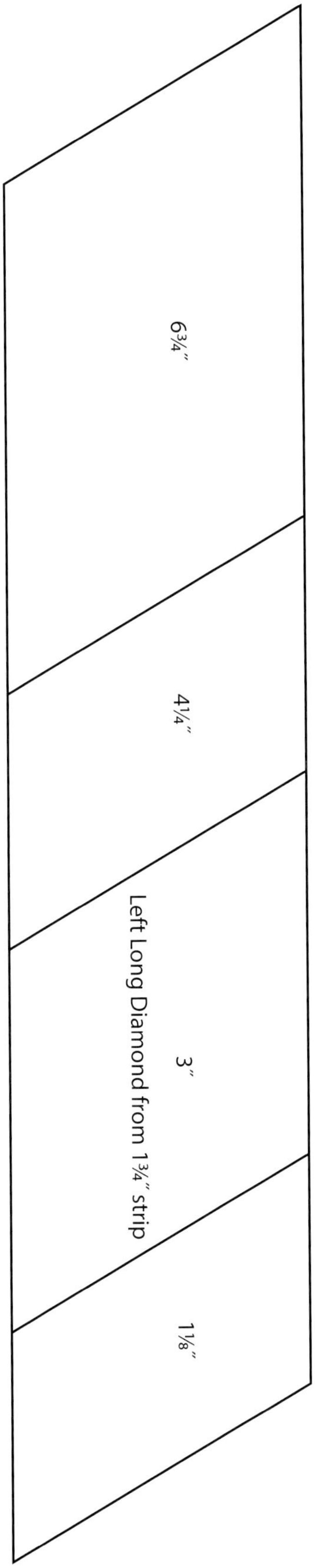
6¾″
4¼″
3″
1⅛″
Left Long Diamond from 1¾″ strip

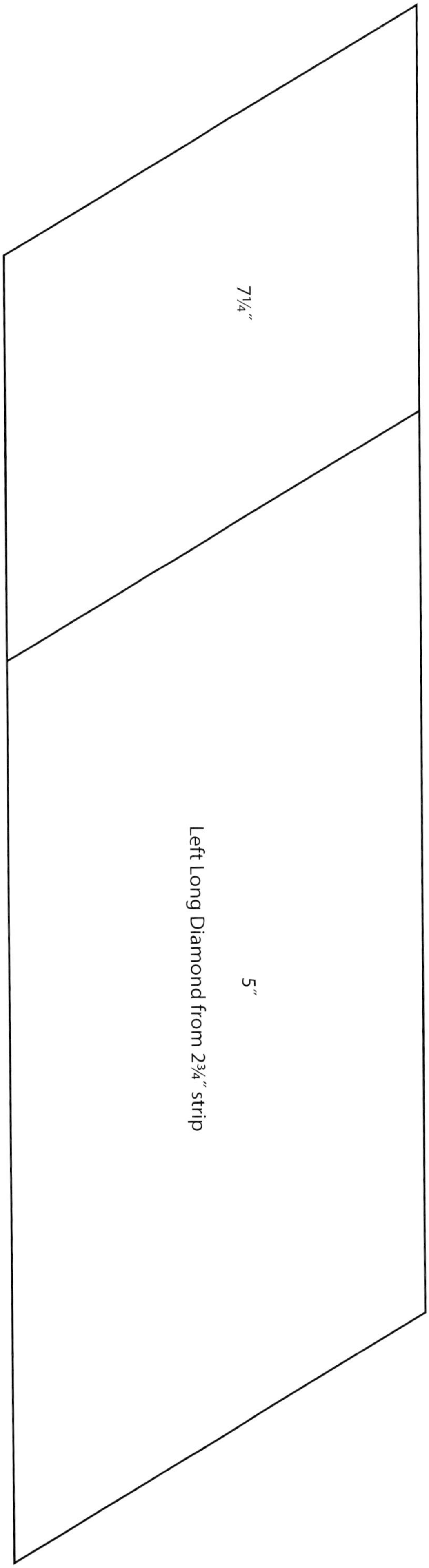
7¼″
5″
Left Long Diamond from 2¾″ strip

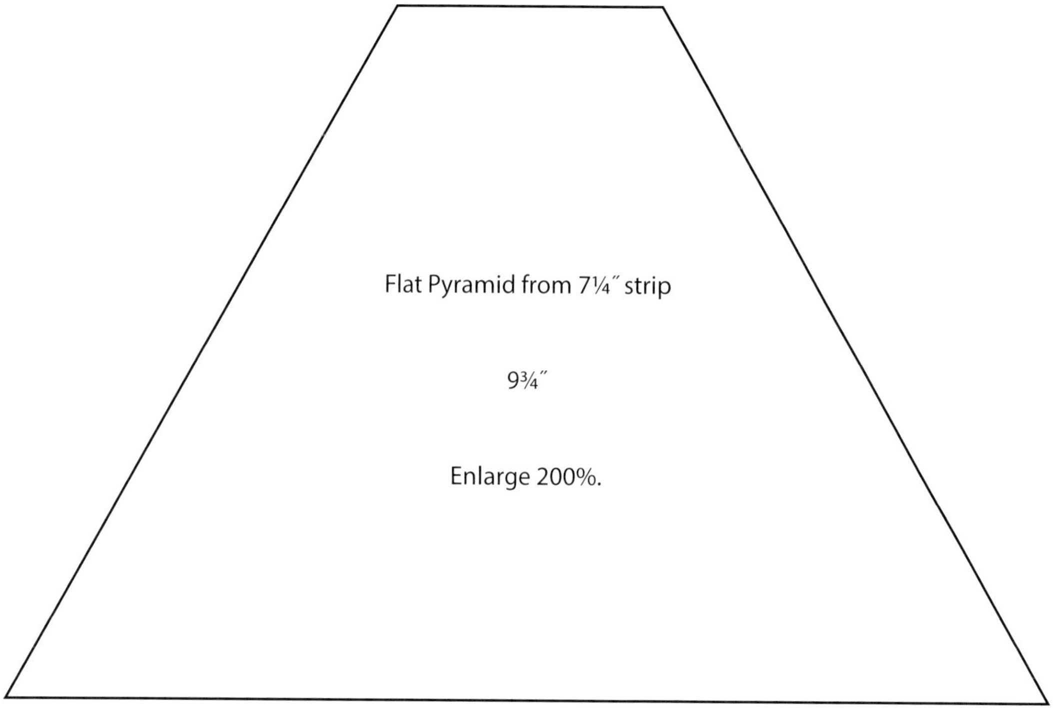
Flat Pyramid from 7¼″ strip
9¾″
Enlarge 200%.

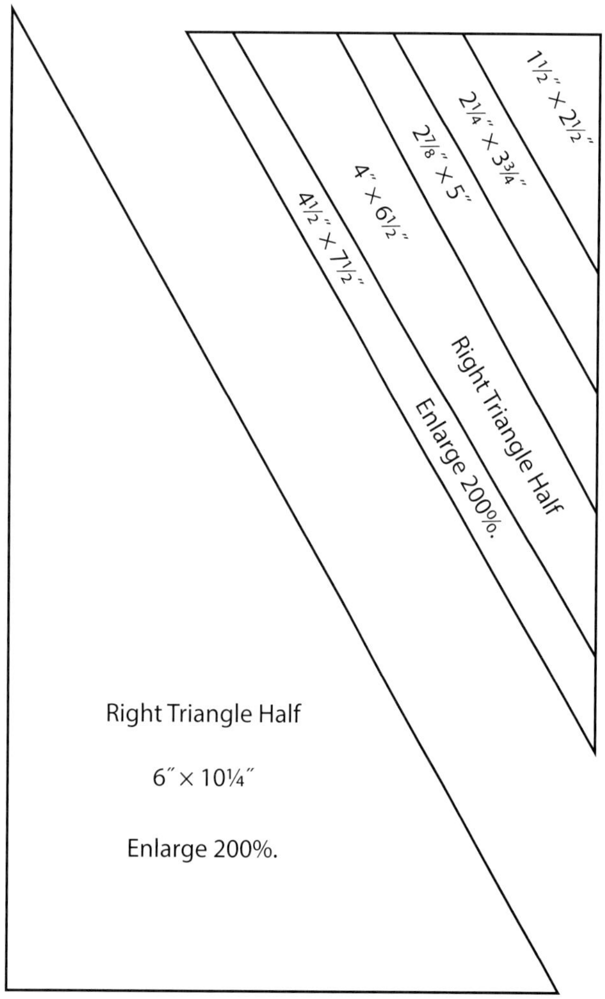
1½″ × 2½″
2¼″ × 3¾″
2⅞″ × 5″
4″ × 6½″
4½″ × 7½″
Right Triangle Half
Enlarge 200%.
Right Triangle Half
6″ × 10¼″
Enlarge 200%.

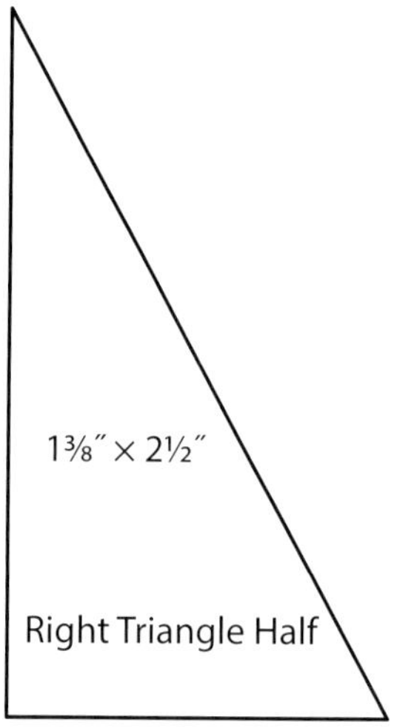
1⅜″ × 2½″
Right Triangle Half

About the Author

Sara Nephew is a quilt designer, author, and teacher and has developed several 60° triangle acrylic rulers. Her quilting career has taken her all over the United States, Canada, and Australia. Sara's quilts have been exhibited in many places. She has been featured in magazine articles, and her quilts have been included in books by other authors.

Sara was born in Milwaukee, Wisconsin, which is also where she grew up, went to high school, and attended college as an art major. She started her career as a commercial jeweler and began to learn diamond setting while continuing her work in painting and cloisonné enameling.

Sara married Dale and moved to Seattle, Washington. She continued to work at home, making original designs of cloisonné and gold and silver jewelry, selling her work at art fairs and by word of mouth. The couple eventually bought three acres in Clearview, a rural area north of Seattle. They planted vegetable gardens and raised chickens, ducks, geese, and turkeys; she milled her own grain, baked bread from scratch, and even made her own soap. Quilting seemed like another "country" kind of thing to do, as well as a way to economically decorate their 1930s home. They had three small children, so quilting—with a sewing machine and lots of beautiful fabric—seemed much more child-friendly than using a jeweler's torch, kiln, and acid. She joined the local guild and began quilting.

Sara started her business, Clearview Triangle, as her multifaceted quilting career took off. In 2006, she retired from the day-to-day operation of running her business and sold her company. However, Sara has not stopped working, creating new quilts, or writing books. Check out Sara's other titles with C&T: *Not Your Grandmother's Log Cabin*, *Wonderful One-Patch Quilts*, and *Stack & Cut Hexagon Quilts*.

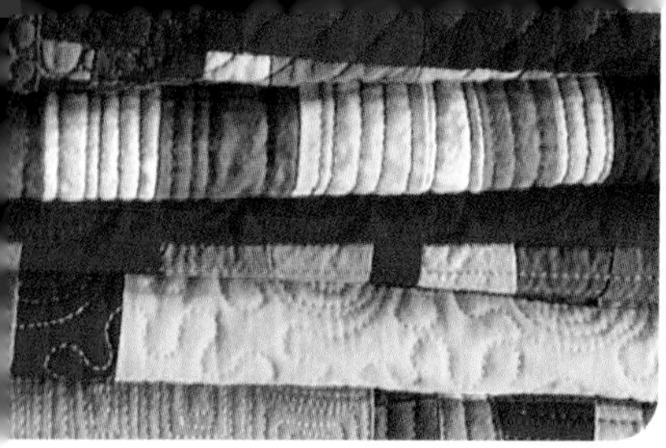
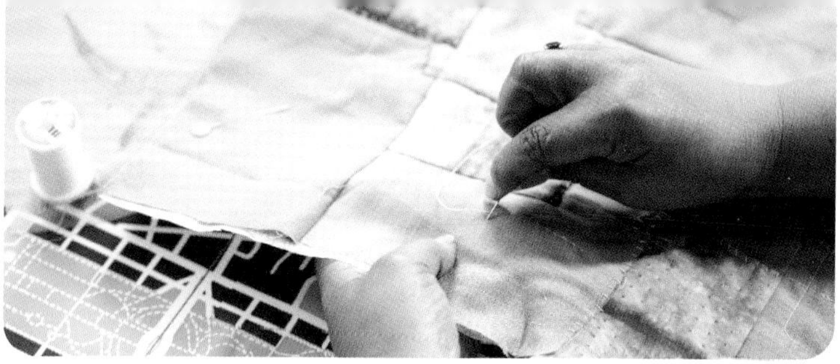

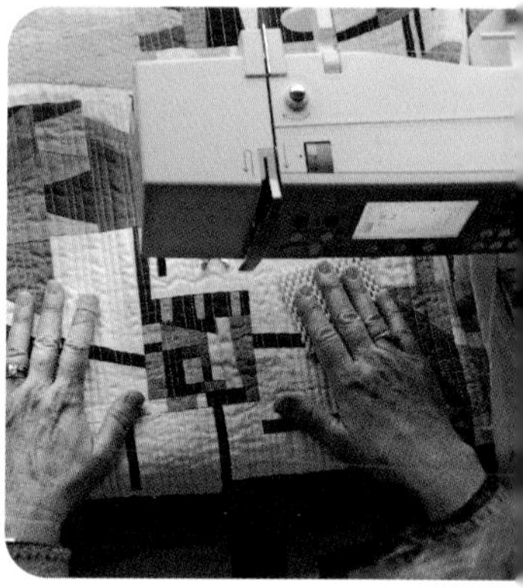